Adolescent Catechesis Resource Manual

Dedicated to:

The women and men who faithfully serve
the Catholic youth of the Church.

SADLIER
Youth Ministry Resources

Adolescent Catechesis Resource Manual

By John Roberto

General Editor of Youth Ministry Series
John Roberto

Official Theological Consultant
Rev. Edward K. Braxton, Ph.D., S.T.D.

Special Consultant
Dr. Thomas H. Groome

Catechetical Consultants
Donald Boyd
James J. DeBoy
Reynolds Ekstrom
Rev. James J. Haddad, S.T.D.
Marina Herrera, Ph.D.

Contents

Nihil Obstat
Reverend James J. Uppena
Censor Deputatus

Imprimatur
✠ Most Reverend Cletus F. O'Donnell
Bishop of Madison
April 5, 1988

The nihil obstat and imprimatur are
official declarations that a book or
pamphlet is free of doctrinal or moral
error. No implication is contained
therein that those who have granted the
nihil obstat and imprimatur agree with
the contents, opinions, or statements
expressed.

Home Office:
9 Pine Street
New York, NY 10005-1002

ISBN: 08215-3000-3
3456789/9876

Preface

Over a decade ago, Catholic Youth Ministry engaged in a process of self-reflection and analysis that resulted in a re-visioning of youth ministry—establishing the goals, principles, and components of a comprehensive, contemporary ministry with youth. *A Vision of Youth Ministry* (USCC, 1976) outlined this comprehensive approach to ministry with youth and became the foundation for a national vision of Catholic Youth Ministry. In the years since the publishing of *A Vision of Youth Ministry,* Catholic Youth Ministry across the United States has experienced tremendous growth. The *Sadlier Youth Ministry Series* is designed to assist this continued growth by offering **Resource Manuals** for adult leaders in ministry with youth and **Catechetical Learning Programs** for youth.

Resource Manuals have been designed to provide leaders with both the foundational understandings and the practical tools they need to create youth ministry programming for each component outlined in the *Vision of Youth Ministry.* The *Sadlier Youth Ministry Series* provides **Resource Manuals** in *Evangelization, Catechesis, Enablement, Family Life, Guidance, Justice and Peace, Service, Prayer, Worship,* and *Retreats.* Each Resource Manual provides foundational essays to familiarize you with that particular component, processes for developing that component, and activities and program models to use in your setting.

The **Catechetical Learning Programs** of the *Sadlier Youth Ministry Series* have been designed using the faith themes of the nationally-accepted *Challenge of Adolescent Catechesis* (NFCYM, 1986). The catechetical programs in the new *Sadlier Youth Ministry Series* offer parish leaders a new opportunity to share with young people the Good News of Jesus Christ and the wisdom of the Catholic Tradition in ways appropriate to their development, culture, language and symbols and in ways that will promote their ongoing growth in faith.

Each catechetical program features the following:

- Six two-hour, fully designed sessions utilizing the shared Christian praxis learning process developed by Dr. Thomas H. Groome;
- Each session is designed to guide the learner through all five movements of shared Christian praxis;
- Each session is a self-contained unit—interdependent with the other five sessions, but not dependent on them;
- Provides on-page activities to allow the adolescents to respond as individuals and also within a peer group to issues affecting their personal growth and religious development;
- Allows catechists and youth to integrate prayer and celebrative aspects of their meetings with the affective, cognitive and behavioral dimensions of the sessions.

For each of the youth booklets, there is a *Teacher's Guide with an Annotated Youth Edition.* Each Guide contains:

- Step-by-Step procedure to the shared Christian praxis approach;
- Clear and precise directions for the catechist to ensure the flow of the session with the adolescents;
- Imaginative and well-tested techniques and activities for use in teaching the session;
- Detailed on-page annotations that supplement and complement the Guide's directions and keeps the focus on the objectives and desired outcomes of the session.

The *Adolescent Catechesis Resource Manual* builds upon *The Challenge of Adolescent Catechesis* by elaborating the foundational understandings of adolescent catechesis and by providing practical resources for developing a catechetical curriculum for adolescents and for designing learning experiences for adolescents.

Introduction

Developments and Directions in Youth Ministry

There has been tremendous growth in Catholic youth ministry since the early 1970s. With the publication in 1976 of *A Vision of Youth Ministry* (USCC, 1976) [abbreviated *Vision* throughout the text], the Catholic Church in the United States began a renewal in ministry with youth that continues today. The *Vision* paper articulated the philosophy, goals, principles, and framework (components) of contemporary youth ministry. This introductory essay seeks to outline the significant trends and developments which have given rise to the current vision of youth ministry in the United States. Secondly, this essay points to future directions by proposing issues that those in Catholic youth ministry need to address. My hope is that this essay can affirm the progress that has been made and challenge us to face the future with courage.

A: The Youth Ministry Agenda Prior to the 1970s

To understand the changes youth ministry would experience in the 1970s, it is important to understand its roots prior to the 1970s. The Church ministered with youth primarily through the programs of the Catholic school, CCD [Confraternity of Christian Doctrine], CYO [Catholic Youth Organization]. Youth work (the term "youth ministry" was not used by the Catholic Church until the 1970s) in this era needs to be understood not as separate programs for youth, but as part of a total ecology or complex of social systems which fostered the growth (personal and spiritual) of young people. Let me give a personal example of what I mean.

I grew up in an extended, Italian (both sides of the family), Catholic family. My family shared with me the values, traditions, and rituals of an Italian Catholic family. Yet they were not alone. My family belonged to an Italian, Catholic parish which served to reinforce the values, traditions, and rituals I learned at home. The parish was an extended family; it seemed like everyone in the parish was related. Through its worship life, community life (especially social events), and programs (for example, CYO) faith was transmitted to the next generation. I also lived in a neighborhood (in a Northeast United States city) where almost everyone was Catholic, and many were Italian, Catholic. When you add up all these factors you can see why there was very little chance that I would grow up to be anything but Catholic (and Italian). To complete this picture, I went to a public elementary school and CCD and then on to Catholic high school. During my high school years I was also active in my parish's CYO. The programs of the CYO, CCD, and Catholic school need to be understood in this context.

This ecology of family, ethnic culture, parish, school, and neighborhood all promoted the same Catholic faith and value system. The programs of the school, CYO, and CCD relied on the supportive context of family and ethnic culture. In fact, these programs *assumed* that all of these social systems were promoting the same faith and value system. When we review the scope of the school, CYO, and CCD through the lens of the 1980s–1990s we might be surprised at how limited the programs were. There was no intention to be comprehensive because all of the other systems were playing a vital role in transmitting faith and values.

The focus of Catholic youth work prior to the 1970s was primarily programmatic and institutional. In parishes, the two main programs were CYO and CCD. CCD, primarily one hour per week, was focused on providing religious (doctrinal) instruction for children and youth who did not attend Catholic schools. CYO (or teen clubs or youth groups) involved a four-fold program of social, athletic, spiritual, and cultural/civic activities. The focus of CYO was on leisure time activities. Describing the focus of CYO, Francis Weldgen writes,

> CYO offered parish youth a diversified program of religious, cultural, social and athletic activities and attempted to bring them closer to the parish community. In 1965 the Advisory Board to the National Director of the Catholic Youth Department (United States Catholic Conference) defined the goals and purpose of CYO as follows: "The ultimate goal of the Catholic Youth Organization is to assist youth and all others in this Apostolate—laity, religious, clergy—to seek the kingdom of God by engaging in temporal affairs by ordering them to the plan of God. The Catholic Youth Apostolate, then, is a participation in the salvific mission of the Church itself . . . thus the immediate goal of the CYO Apostolate is the consecration to God of the leisure hours of youth and the sanctification of youth through a well-balanced leisure time program."[1]

In the context of family, the parish community and ethnic culture, the limited focus of CCD and CYO were effective. CCD and CYO relied on

these contexts to play a vital role in transmitting faith and values. Like the programs of the Catholic school, CYO and CCD could only be seen in this total ecology. Without the broader transmitting of faith and values, youth programs would cease to be effective. This, in part, explains the decline of youth programs in the 1970s.

B: Agenda for the 1970s

The conditions surrounding the appearance of youth ministry in the Roman Catholic community in the early 1970s were reflective of the enormous changes underway in the Church and in society, particularly the youth culture, and its global context. The systems that provided a context for youth work in the 1960s began to change—family, parish, ethnic culture, and neighborhood. What had been assumed or taken for granted in youth programming was also changing. This dual transformation meant that much of the programming that relied on such systems began to decline—declining participation from youth who did not want to join "clubs" or go to "classes," outmoded programming that no longer responded to youth needs, and dwindling numbers of leaders who would work with youth. On the one hand, the older forms of youth work were breaking down. On the other hand, the question arose, what would the break-through to new forms of youth ministry look like?

The break-through began by the mid-1970s. New creativity began to respond to the declining picture with a new vision and direction for youth work. New research on church youth began to surface. One of the early studies, *Five Cries of Youth* (1974) by Merton Strommen gave youth work an empirical foundation. The new "theology of ministry" and "theology of church" that were emerging in the post-Vatican II era gave theological substance and a new vocabulary to youth work.

Youth work became more person-centered, rather than program centered, and more relational and community-based. The emphasis in the early 1970s was on reaching out to youth who were no longer participating in church programs, trying to build relationships with them, to create community with them, and to develop programs that focused on *their needs.* A hallmark of these early efforts was the emphasis on integrating programs that had once been separate. The framework of *To Teach as Jesus Did* (NCCB, 1972), offered such a focus: Community—Message—Service.

> The educational mission of the Church as an integrated ministry embracing three interlocking dimensions: the message revealed by God (*didache*) which the Church proclaims; fellowship in the life of the Holy Spirit (*koinonia*); service to the Christian community and the entire human community (*diakonia*) [paragraph #14].[2]

This integration was happening at both the vision level and at the pastoral level. Marisa Guerin writes,

> Both religious education/catechesis and youth activities were expanding beyond traditional limits to incorporate an awareness of the humanistic, interpersonal, affective dimension of coming to faith. Youth retreats were the common ground for this renewal. In the ferment, the orderly boundaries that had once separated and regulated the relations, goals, and methods of religious education, CYO, schools, Scouts, camping, etc. became porous. There was a sense of belonging together somehow, and there were also a lot of partisan feelings about whose tradition, procedures, and leadership made sense for the future. . . .[3]

It was out of this development, in vision and practice, that the ground was being prepared for *A Vision of Youth Ministry* in 1976. Once again, Guerin summarizes this process when she writes,

The theme that emerged was captured in the phrase, "youth ministry." Those two words symbolized a new and different relation among those who care for the youth of our Church. However, like any symbol, the term "youth ministry" tended to lose precision of meaning. It became impossible to know with any certainty what different people meant by the term. The vision paper was a nationally supported activity intended to clarify the theme. With a process that began in 1975 at the (then) National Advisory Board meeting, leaders and practitioners from across the country engaged in a dialogue that produced three successive drafts of the statement. The dialogue was cross-disciplinary, involving youth activities persons, religious educators, and schools personnel.

Although the explicit aim of the process was *agreement* on a definition of youth ministry, the actual, more profound, result was the *alignment* of many individual visions with a common language and focus. Alignment is much more powerful than formal agreements to evoke joint action, especially over large geographic and cultural distances in a pluralistic Church. In this case, thousands of people had become part of a living, evolving consensus, reducing the need for formal agreements.

Once it was published, the *Vision of Youth Ministry* paper became the central theme and reference point for all the parties involved in the renewal that we have come to know as youth ministry practice in the Church. Ironically, the paper did not describe what the changed praxis of the future would look like, it said little about how the change would occur, and it tended to raise more questions than it answered. What it did offer was an image (the Emmaus story), an articulated priority on relational, community-based ministry, and a set of goals, principles and components to serve as guideposts for re-ordering action.[4]

A Vision of Youth Ministry offered an integrated, comprehensive vision of ministry with youth. It transcended the narrower programs like CYO, CCD/religious education and youth group. It mapped out a ministerial framework that attends to a wider set of youth needs. It is to this vision that we now turn.

The Vision of Youth

From the outset the *Vision* paper made clear its ecclesial focus: "As one among many ministries of the Church, youth ministry must be understood in terms of the mission and ministry of the whole Church" (p.3). The focus is clearly ministerial. "The Church's mission is threefold: to proclaim the good news of salvation, offer itself as a group of people transformed by the Spirit into a community of faith, hope, and love, and to bring God's justice and love to others through service in its individual, social, and political dimensions" (p.3). This threefold mission formed the basis of the framework or components of youth ministry: Word (evangelization and catechesis), Worship, Community, Justice and Service, Guidance and Healing, Enablement, and Advocacy.

Dimensions of Youth Ministry

The *Vision* paper described a broad concept of ministry with youth using four dimensions. Youth Ministry is . . .

To youth—responding to youth's varied needs

With youth—working with adults to fulfill their common responsibility for the Church's mission

By youth—exercising their own ministry to others: peers, community, world

For youth—interpreting the needs of youth, especially in areas of injustice and acting on behalf of or with youth for a change in the systems which create injustice.

Goals

The *Vision* paper outlined two goals for the Church's ministry with youth:

1. Youth Ministry works for the total personal and spiritual growth of each young person.
2. Youth Ministry seeks to draw young people to responsible participation in the life, mission, and work of the faith community (p. 7).

The first goal emphasizes *becoming*—focusing on the *personal level* of human existence. The second goal emphasizes *belonging*—focusing on the *interpersonal* or *communal dimension* of human existence. In light of the Church's priority upon justice and peace, and the mission of the Church to transform society (for example, *Brothers and Sisters to Us,* NCCB, 1979; *The Challenge of Peace,* NCCB, 1983; and *Economic Justice for All,* NCCB, 1986), it would be appropriate to consider adding a third goal. This third goal would challenge youth ministry to empower young people to become aware of the social responsibilities of the Christian faith—the call to live and work for justice and peace. Youth ministry needs to empower young people with the knowledge and skills to transform the unjust structures of society so that these transformed structures promote justice, respect human dignity, promote human rights, and build peace. This third goal emphasizes *transforming*—focusing on the public or *social structural* level of human existence. This third goal gives a greater comprehensiveness to youth ministry.

A Dual Focus

Youth ministry has a dual focus. It is a ministry *within* the community of faith—ministering to believing youth and *to* the wider society—reaching out to serve youth in our society. While the experience of the past decade has emphasized ministry within the community, youth ministry needs to broaden its focus to address the social situation and needs of all youth in society. It is a challenge of the future.

Contexts

An underdeveloped but increasingly important section of the *Vision* paper is the contexts of youth ministry. "In all places, youth ministry occurs within a given social, cultural, and religious context which shapes the specific form of the ministry" (p. 10). This contextual approach seeks to view young people as part of a number of social systems which impact on their growth, values, and faith, rather than as isolated individuals. Among these systems are the family, society, the dominant culture, youth culture, ethnic culture, school, and local church community. In the last several years, youth ministry has become much more aware of the impact of these systems.

For example, research and pastoral experience point to the realization that a ministry with youth is a ministry with their families. First, parishes/schools are beginning to see that an essential aspect of their ministry is encouraging and supporting the role of parents, involving families in parish/school youth programming, and providing programs and services for parents (and youth) that respond to their needs. Secondly, youth ministry has become more aware of the cultural impact of media upon young people (for example, rock music, music videos, advertising, TV) and has established programs to raise young people's awareness of this influence. The increasing importance of these contexts or systems points to a direction for ongoing growth in youth ministry.

Components

The framework (or components) describe distinct aspects for developing a comprehensive, integrated ministry with youth. Briefly, these components include:

Evangelization—reaching out to young people who are uninvolved in the life of the community and inviting them into a relationship with Jesus and the Christian community. Evangelization involves proclaiming the Good News of Jesus through programs and relationships.

Catechesis—promoting a young person's growth in Christian faith through the kind of teaching and learning that emphasizes understanding, reflection, and transformation. This is accomplished through systematic, planned and intentional programming (curriculum) (see *The Challenge of Adolescent Catechesis,* NFCYM, 1986).

Worship—assisting young people in deepening their relationship with Jesus through the development of a personal prayer life; and providing a variety of prayer and worship experiences with youth to deepen and celebrate their relationship with Jesus in a caring Christian community; involving young people in the sacramental life of the Church.

Community Life—building Christian community with youth through programs and relationships which promote openness, trust, valuing the person, cooperation, honesty, taking responsibility, and willingness to serve; creating a climate where young people can grow and share their struggles, questions, and joys with other youth and adults; helping young people feel like a valued part of the Church.

Guidance and Healing—providing youth with sources of support and counsel as they face personal problems and pressures (for example, family problems, peer pressure, substance abuse, suicide) and decide on careers and important life decisions; providing appropriate support and guidance for youth during times of stress and crisis; helping young people deal with the problems they face and the pressures people place on them; developing a better understanding of their parents and learning how to communicate with them.

Justice, Peace, and Service—guiding young people in developing a Christian social consciousness and a commitment to a life of justice and peace through educational programs and service/action involvement; infusing the concepts of justice and peace into all youth ministry relationships and programming.

Enablement—developing, supporting, and utilizing the leadership abilities and personal gifts of youth and adults in youth ministry, empowering youth for ministry with their peers; developing a leadership team to organize and coordinate the ministry with youth.

Advocacy—interpreting the needs of youth: personal, family, and social especially in areas of injustices towards or oppression of youth, and acting with or on behalf of youth for a change in the systems which create injustice; giving young people a voice and empowering them to address the social problems that they face.

A Collaborative Ministry

For *A Vision of Youth Ministry* to be realized there must be collaboration among all those who minister with youth. The paper states:

> No one aspect of youth ministry is independent of others; they are all interdependent elements of a unified total vision. The multifaceted nature of youth ministry requires a process of collaboration among all persons involved in it, rather than fragmentation or competition. . . . Part of the vision of youth ministry is to present to youth the richness of the person of Christ, which perhaps exceeds the ability of one person to capture, but which might be effective by the collective ministry of the many persons who make up the Church.

> In all of these developing models (parish, school, diocesan), however, the process of dialogue, collaboration and joint planning is the key to ending fragmentation and restoring a sense of balance to the ministry with youth (p. 24).

No one program, be it CYO, religious education or youth group, no one organizational model and no one minister working alone can capture the totality of youth ministry. It is a comprehensive, multifaceted, collaborative ministry.

C: The Contribution of the Vision of Youth

Marisa Guerin captures successfully the power and impact of the *Vision* paper,

> The *Vision of Youth Ministry* has the power to re-weave into whole cloth the separated strands of programs and bureaucracies of the Church. It is not an *anti*-organizational vision, but a vision of an *enspirited* organization. The vision provides us with a language of connection with which to view the pastoral work that is the obligation of the Church community to its youth.[5]

There has been real progress and growth on several fronts since 1976. Here are several highlights of this growth.

1 **A changed relation between formerly separate avenues of church life into a conceptually integrated whole.**

More and more parishes and Catholic high schools are developing a comprehensive ministry with youth that integrates the components of youth ministry in a holistic approach. For parishes, the attention to youth's needs and a comprehensive approach has meant an increase in youth participation in youth programs and parish life. For Catholic high schools a more comprehensive approach has meant attentiveness to a broader range of youth needs and the development of a vision of the entire school, its programs and people, as a ministering community.

2 **A set of structures and organizations able to provide the right kind of leadership and resources to the field. There is increased collaboration in ministry with youth at all levels of Church.**

3 A new generation of young people and of adult volunteers, who take the concept of personal, communal ministry as a given, and who have become educated in the theology and behavioral sciences that support solid youth ministry work.

The number of professional and paraprofessional parish coordinators of youth ministry and of high school campus ministers has grown dramatically in the 1980s. Increasing numbers of parish and Catholic high schools are hiring coordinators or calling forth local leaders to coordinate youth ministry efforts. These coordinators, salaried and volunteer, possess higher levels of experience, competence, and training in youth ministry. There is an increasing priority by dioceses and universities to provide quality ministry education programs for coordinators of youth ministry. This emphasis on training has resulted in a growing trend toward credentialing coordinators with degrees (B.A. or M.A.) or certificates in youth ministry.

4 The increasing emphasis at all levels of youth ministry on preparing youth for leadership and peer ministry. This emphasis upon youth as leaders and peer ministers is a significant change from simply viewing them as the "recipients" of a ministry *to*; it calls for actively engaging them in leadership and ministry. Church and society are benefiting from the energy, commitment, and faith of youth.

5 The direction given to adolescent catechesis within a comprehensive ministry with youth by the publication in 1986 of *The Challenge of Adolescent Catechesis.* Developed collaboratively by four national organizations, *The Challenge* articulated the foundations, aims, principles, and faith themes for adolescent catechesis. It provided a solid foundation for the future growth of adolescent catechesis within *A Vision of Youth Ministry.*

D: Looking Ahead: An Agenda for the Second Decade of the Vision of Youth Ministry

What are some of the issues and concerns that youth ministry must confront in the second decade? While it would be presumptuous to offer a definitive list, the following issues and concerns seem to surface consistently in youth ministry writings, at conferences and gatherings, and in discussions with youth ministry leaders in dioceses, schools, and parishes. The following analysis is offered as a guide so that we may discern the next steps in the journey. Focusing on these issues does not mean that we leave behind the tasks outlined earlier in this essay. Those trends need to be continued and strengthened. Focusing on the following issues means we will continue to grow and confront new challenges, being faithful to the ministry that God has entrusted to us.

1. **Justice:**

   There is a great opportunity today to address with youth the pressing questions of justice and peace in our country and in our world. With the *Challenge of Peace* and *Economic Justice for All,* the Catholic bishops of the United States have spoken clearly about the priority of peace and justice for the Church. In 1986, Catholic Relief Services and the National Federation for Catholic Youth Ministry sponsored a National Symposium on Justice and Peace to explore foundations in theology, church teaching, spirituality, social analysis, and to develop education models, among which are action and infusion models. (Action model promotes hands-on experiences for youth, for example, working in a soup kitchen; infusion model develops lesson plans using concepts connected with justice and peace and weaves them into the regular curriculum.) The challenge to make justice and peace (education, action, and infusion) a constitutive part of our ministry with youth must absorb our energies in the second decade if we are to be faithful to Good News and to our youth.

2. Family Ministry:

The rapidly changing face of the family and the importance of the family system in nurturing the faith growth of young people, calls out for new initiatives with parents, with the family system, with parent and teens on issues that affect both of them. Every parish/ school can become more family-sensitive (i.e. a supportive system for family life) by offering parent programs/ services and by designing its ministries/programs, schedules, etc., with a family perspective. In particular there are at least three kinds of programming that can be developed:

a. Programs specifically designed for parents.

1. educational experiences that communicate information on adolescent growth, develop skills for communication and for parenting;
2. parent support groups (especially for single and blended family parents and for those experiencing divorce or separation);
3. educational programs contemporary Church teachings.

b. Programs for parents and adolescents.

One way to integrate parents into the youth ministry is to design certain programs to include or incorporate parent sessions. A course on sexuality (a great course to involve parents) might follow this sequence: a parents-only session, followed by three youth sessions, another parents-only session, then three more youth sessions, and finally a parent-teen closing session. Other possibilities for parent-teen programming include:

1. family activities and programs which build communication, trust, and closeness;
2. parent-teen programs that discuss moral values and promote discussion;
3. worship and Scripture resources for parents to use in the home;
4. justice and service projects that involve the whole family (perhaps at regularly scheduled times during the year);
5. parent-teen retreat experiences; and
6. home-based advent and lenten programs (as individual families or clusters).

c. Parallel programs for adults and adolescents.

There is a critical need to develop and offer programs for parents which parallel the programs offered the young people. Parents could take an adult course (morality or Scripture), while their son or daughter was participating in an adolescent course on the same topic; or a program on communication that complements their son or daughter's program offerings.

As with so many of these issues, we will need to collaborate with family researchers, family ministers, family social service agencies if we are to meet adequately the challenge.

3. Multicultural Youth Ministry and Catechesis:

In our multicultural society and Church, ministry with youth must develop approaches for ministering with various cultures, for cross cultural ministry, and for infusing and celebrating a multicultural perspective in all youth ministry. The reality of a multicultural Church and society has yet to make a serious impact on our ministry with youth. Those of the dominant culture tend to see it as another issue which is at the periphery of their lives and ministry. Such an attitude could not be further from the truth. There is a widespread lack of "cultural literacy" among ministers and it is a major problem. Marina Herrera describes how youth ministry needs to be multi-cultural:

> I am firmly convinced that youth ministry must have a clear connection with cultural anthropology but not merely with reference to minority cultures but to the cultural patterns and understandings of the dominant groups as well .... youth ministry should be multi-cultural in two clearly distinct and yet interrelated dimensions: 1) youth ministry must concern itself with the needs of minority youth; and 2) youth ministry must also have a direct multi-cultural dimension when intended for youth from the dominant culture.[6]

The author has set out two tasks for youth ministry in a multi-cultural society. Youth ministry must take its clues from the cultural context as well as the psychological, political or educational ones. Using these twin tasks as an evaluative tool one can see that we have much work to do. How effectively do we engage in ministry with minority youth and respond to their personal, familial, social, and institutional needs? How effectively do our training programs prepare us for this ministry? How will the church-at-large work to find the money and resources to support youth ministers and youth ministries in minority parishes and communities? How effectively do we integrate the reality of our multi-cultural society in our programs for youth and leaders of the dominant culture so that they may see the riches of all cultures and live their lives accordingly? Youth Ministry in the second decade must take the needs of minority youth and the education of the dominant culture seriously if we are to respond to the challenge of living and ministering in a multi-cultural Church and society.

4. Cultural and Media:

Michael Warren and other writers on youth ministry have begun to raise the consciousness of youth ministers and religious educators to the educational task of raising young people's consciousness about the impact of the dominant culture, and especially the media, on their identity, values, and faith. It is becoming quite clear that there is often a confrontation between the dominant culture's vision of life and the Christian vision of life. We need to teach young people to analyze critically the cultural vision of life, to contrast it with the Christian vision of life and to learn how to resist the cultural influences.

As we become more aware of the world young people live in, its powerful impact on their lives, and of the educational processes that promote freedom, we will be able to confront the challenge. Efforts toward developing the critical thinking skills of youth

and of bringing the culture, especially the media, into our educational and pastoral efforts remains a task to be undertaken by youth ministers.

5. Youth-at-Risk:

Experts estimate that approximately 25% of all adolescents are at serious risk in our society, brought on by such problems as substance abuse, unemployment, teenage sexual activity and pregnancy, high school dropouts, suicide, and adolescent stress. So much of the renewal of youth ministry has been focused internally—on ministry *within* the community and this has been and will continue to be important work as more and more parishes and schools renew their ministry with youth. However, this internal renewal needs to be balanced by an equal concern for ministry to the concerns and needs of youth in our society. Youth ministry in the second decade will need to take seriously its mission to the social situation of young people in our society. How can a school or parish confront these societal problems? In addition to understanding the problems and surveying available resources, these problems call for us to collaborate with experts in order to create new approaches, new directions.

Consider the plight of youth from poor families in inner cities or in rural areas. They feel a deep sense of hopelessness about their lives and future. They suffer from poor quality education, unemployment and/or underemployment, inadequate housing, poor nutrition. The Federal budget cuts have only made their plight and their future more difficult. How does youth ministry respond to their needs, especially when almost all of the salaried coordinators of youth ministry work in wealthier urban or suburban parishes? What can be done when the problems seem so complex and overwhelming, when the resources seem so scarce? One of the measures of our effectiveness in youth ministry will be our response to the needs of youth who suffer from injustice and poverty.

We will need to become more proficient in advocacy and be able to collaborate with others in creating new responses.

6. Broadening the Scope of Youth Ministry:

There is a growing movement to apply the comprehensive framework of youth ministry to minister with younger adolescents (10-14 year olds) and early young adult (18-22/25 year olds). Much of youth ministry has concentrated on the particular needs of high school aged youth. There is a growing awareness in youth ministry leaders that we need to minister to a broader age range of youth. With more and more research on the needs of early adolescence, youth ministry leaders can now build a ministry to the young adolescent modeled on the framework of youth ministry. Such a comprehensive ministry is long overdue and complements the progress we have made in youth ministry.

Young adult ministry, which has made significant gains in the past decade, deserves the attention of youth ministry leaders. In what ways can we collaborate with young adult ministry leaders, bringing the vision and experience of youth ministry to bear on young adult ministry? In what ways can parish coordinators of youth ministry utilize their youth ministry efforts as a way to give birth to a comprehensive ministry with young adults? In many places, youth ministry can be the catalyst for a ministry with young adults.

Let me conclude with the prophetic voice of Hispanic youth from the III Encuentro process, which captures so well what I have been trying to say about the challenges for the second decade. These words of youth are the new horizon for youth ministry.

As Hispanic young people, as members of the Catholic Church we wish to raise our prophetic voice in order to announce the values of the Gospel, to denounce sin, to invite all youth to struggle for the Kingdom of God.

First of all, we announce the option for peace as against violence (Mt 26:51; 2 Cor 5:18); for love as against injustice (Jn 15:17); for good as against evil (Dt 30:15); for the family as a fundamental value through which faith is transmitted (Eph 6:4); and for maintaining one's own culture.

Likewise, we denounce materialism, which leads us to believe that the important thing in life is to have more and more in contrast to the teachings of the Gospel (Mt 6:25-30; *Populorum Progressio,* no. 19).

We denounce the injustice and oppression that Latin America suffers as a result of the cultural, economic, military, and political intervention of wealthy nations.

We denounce the hunger and poverty that our people, with whom Jesus identifies, suffer (Mt 25:31), the violence (Mt 26:52), and the arms race (*The Challenge of Peace,* no. 204); we are opposed to any use of nuclear weapons (*Ibid,* no. 215).

We denounce the Melting Pot theory and make an option for learning the culture of this country without forgetting our own. (*Evangelii Nuntiandi,* no. 20). We denounce abortion, the abuse of drugs and alcohol, and the negative and manipulative influence of commercial propaganda that creates false needs.

We do not just denounce these injustices, we also feel ourselves called to struggle for peace in the world, to live a more simple life style in solidarity with our poor brothers and sisters, and to reach out beyond our nationalities, races, languages, and socioeconomic levels so as to be really one Catholic family.

Let us, likewise, contribute our joy and enthusiasm to the liturgical style of the ecclesial community of the United States. Let us be aware that we can change the world with our way of life today.[7]

Notes

1. *Hope for Decade,* (Washington, DC: National CYO Federation, 1981), pp. 3-4.

2. *To Teach as Jesus Did,* (Washington, DC: NCCB, United States Catholic Conference, 1973), pp. 4-5.

3. Marisa Guerin, "Beyond the Vision," *Occasional Paper #12.* (Naugatuck, CT: Center for Youth Ministry Development, 1987), pp. 2-3.

4. *Ibid,* pp. 4-5

Select Bibliography

Bagley, Ronald. Editor. *Young Adult Ministry—A Book of Readings.* Naugatuck, CT: Center for Youth Ministry Development, 1987.

Bowman, Thea. Editor. *Families—Black and Catholic, Catholic and Black.* Washington, DC: USCC/Department of Education, 1985.

The Challenge of Adolescent Catechesis—Maturing in Faith. Washington, DC: NFCYM Publications, 1986.

The Challenge of Peace. Washington, DC: NCCB/USCC Publishing, 1983.

Economic Justice for All. Washington, DC: NCCB/USCC Publishing, 1986.

Faith and Culture. Washington, DC: USCC/Department of Education, 1987/

Farel, Anita. *Early Adolescence and Religion.* Carrboro, NC: Center for Early Adolescence, 1982.

Fox, Zeni, et al. *Leadership for Youth Ministry.* Winona, MN: St. Mary's Press. 1984.

Guerin, Marisa. "Beyond the Vision." in *Occasional Paper #12.* Naugatuck, CT: Center for Youth Ministry Development. 1987.

Harris, Maria. *Portrait of Youth Ministry.* New York, NY: Paulist Press, 1981.

Hershey, Terry. *Young Adult Ministry.* Loveland, CO: Group Books, 1986.

Jones, Nathan. *Sharing the Old, Old Story—Educational Ministry in the Black Community.* Winona, MN: St. Mary's Press, 1982.

Kimball, Don. *Power and Presence—A Theology of Relationships.* San Francisco, CA Harper and Row, 1987.

5. *Ibid,* p. 6.

6. Marina Herrera, "Toward Multi-cultural Youth Ministry," in *Readings in Youth Ministry* Volume 1, (Washington, DC: NFCYM Publications, 1986), p. 90.

7. *Prophetic Voices—The Document on the Process of the III Encuentro Nacional Hispano de Pastoral,* Secretariat for Hispanic Affairs, (Washington, DC: United States Catholic Conference, 1986), p. 12.

Lefstein, Leah, et al. *3:00-6:00 P.M.: Young Adolescents at Home and in the Community.* Carrboro, NC: Center for Early Adolescence, 1982.

Ng, David. *Youth in the Community of Disciples.* Valley Forge, PA: Judson Press, 1984.

A Pastoral Plan for Young Adult Ministry. Washington, DC: USCC, 1980.

Rice, Wayne. *Junior High Ministry.* Grand Rapids, MI: Zondervan, 1987.

Roberto, John. Compiler. *Readings in Youth Ministry.* Washington, DC: NFCYM Publications, 1986.

Shaheen, David. *Growing a Junior High Ministry.* Loveland, CO: Group Books, 1986.

Shelton, Charles. *Adolescent Spirituality.* Chicago, IL: Loyola University Press. 1983.

Strommen, Merton and Irene. *Five Cries of Parents.* San Francisco, CA: Harper & Row, 1985.

Warren, Michael. *Youth, Gospel, Liberation.* San Francisco: Harper and Row. 1987.

_____ . *Youth and the Future of the Church.* San Francisco: Harper and Row. 1982.

_____ . Editor. *Resources in Youth Ministry.* Winona, MN: St. Mary's Press. 1987.

Vision of Youth Ministry. Washington, DC: Department of Education. USCC. 1976.

Chapter 1 — Adolescent Catechesis Today

A new day has dawned in the ministry of adolescent catechesis and with it new hope and new challenges. With the publication in 1986 of *The Challenge of Adolescent Catechesis* [abbreviated *The Challenge*], a fresh vision has emerged to articulate the aim, process, guiding principles, and faith themes for catechesis with younger and older adolescents. Developed collaboratively by the National Federation for Catholic Youth Ministry, the National Conference of Diocesan Directors of Religious Education, and the National Catholic Education Association, the document reflects a national vision and direction for adolescent catechesis. *The Challenge* is both visionary and practical. It provides a well-rounded view of catechesis that will affirm and challenge our present understanding and practice.

A Definition

The Challenge presents an understanding and practice of catechesis as a "systematic, planned, and intentional pastoral activity. This activity is directed toward the kind of teaching and learning which emphasizes growth in Christian faith through understanding, reflection, and transformation" (p. 5).

The first key element in this understanding is the nature of catechesis as systematic, planned and intentional. There are many ways in which faith is fostered through family, parish, ethnic culture and a comprehensive ministry with youth. Adolescent catechesis contributes to the faith growth of youth by providing a systematic and planned learning program. This systematic and planned approach is what is often needed in parish youth ministry efforts. While a systematic and planned approach is the strength of Catholic school programs, the broader ministerial context (for example, campus ministry) for adolescent faith growth is often needed.

Equally important is the second key element—teaching and learning which promotes faith growth through understanding, reflection, and transformation. All too often, catechesis has only promoted growth through understanding. Developing an understanding of the Catholic Christian Story (our Tradition) and Vision (the Reign of God) is an important task for catechesis. However, understanding needs to be complemented by reflection and transformation. Critical reflection upon the Story and Vision and the ways the Story and Vision affirms and critiques our life experience and values/beliefs, our culture and society is essential for catechesis. Reflection helps youth find a vocabulary for their belief, to examine it, and to own it. Reflection helps young people integrated the Story and Vision into their lives. A catechesis which promotes transformation fosters ongoing conversion, affecting our heads, hearts, and lifestyles. It enables young people to live the Story and Vision at all levels of human existence—the personal, the interpersonal, and the social/political.

The Aim of Adolescent Catechesis

The primary aim of adolescent catechesis is "to sponsor youth toward maturity in Catholic Christian faith as a living reality. We adults guide, challenge, affirm and encourage youth in their journey toward maturing in faith" (p. 8). The key insight, articulated in this aim, is that adolescent catechesis is the process of journeying with young people toward increasing maturity as Catholic Christians. This "journeying with youth" means that catechists share not only the Christian Story and Vision but also their own journey of faith. By guiding, challenging, affirming and encouraging, catechists enable youth to make their faith a living reality in their lives.

Two tasks are central to the aim of adolescent catechesis: "to foster in youth a communal identity as Catholic Christians and to help them develop their own personal faith identity" (p. 8). The first task calls us to "present the faith convictions and values of the Catholic Christian tradition and invite adolescents to adopt and own these values and convictions" (p. 8). The second task, involves us in helping "adolescents respond to God in faith, in prayer, in values, and behavior" (p. 8). This second task requires that we help young people give birth to their own faith knowing and faith response. These twin tasks may seem to pull the catechist in two different directions. In fact, they complement each other. These twin tasks of adolescent catechesis, communal identity and personal faith identity, need to permeate all of our catechesis with youth.

Principles of Adolescent Catechesis

The ten principles articulated in *The Challenge* give adolescent catechesis a fresh spirit and specific focus. Here is a brief overview of each principle. As you read them, reflect on how your catechetical ministry embodies these principles.

Foundational Principles

The following foundational principles describe the key understandings that shape adolescent catechesis:

1 **Adolescent catechesis is situated within the lifelong developmental process of faith growth and of ongoing catechesis. The entire catechetical effort is committed to the continuing faith growth of the individual.**

When we act on the principle of lifelong catechesis, we are challenged to adjust our expectations for what can be accomplished in adolescent catechesis and to plan our curriculum as part of a lifelong approach. It is not realistic to expect that catechesis for seven or eight years of the person's life will be able to fulfill all religious needs. We need to focus on

the unique contribution of adolescent catechesis to the lifelong catechetical effort.

2 **Adolescent catechesis fosters Catholic Christian faith in three dimensions: trusting, believing, and doing.**

Faith is above all a gift. It is a God-given invitation to all people to share in God's love and life. This invitation or call lovingly urges, but never forces, us to accept. Our response to the gift of faith is a personal encounter with God in Jesus Christ, an encounter that transforms our way of life. It is a choice made in freedom. Genuine faith is a total response of the whole person—mind, heart, and will. This holistic approach to faith, dominating much of contemporary theology, is the foundation for all catechesis.

This holistic approach to faith, challenges us to provide more than systematic instruction on doctrine. Although understanding the tradition is essential, it is equally essential to experience the building of trusting relationships, the participatory experience of religious community and celebration, and the living out of the faith that does justice. This comprehensive vision of faith will mean added attention to the affective, the imaginative, and the action/lifestyle elements of the response of faith.

We are challenged to provide our catechesis in an atmosphere that is inviting and free. This environment needs to be characterized by warmth, trust, acceptance and care so that young people can hear and respond to God's call. It also needs to be characterized by freedom—to search and question, to express one's own point of view, to respond in faith. We cannot force the response in faith.

We are challenged to plan our curriculum and each learning program so that we help adolescents develop a deeper relationship with Jesus and the community (trusting), deepen and expand their understanding of the Christian Story and Vision (believing), and live more faithfully the call to justice and a life of loving service (doing).

3 **Adolescent catechesis supports and encourages the role of the family and in particular the role of the parent in the faith growth of the young person and involves the parent in formulation of an adolescent catechesis curriculum and in programs to strengthen their parenting role.**

We are challenged to extend our ministry to parents through support and education, as well as involve them in developing/improving a curriculum. In their book, *Five Cries of Parents,* Merton and Irene Strommen identify several sources of family strength, drawn from research and experience, that can greatly help young people grow in faith:

1. Understanding, Affirming Parents

These parents understand themselves and the changes typical of the adolescent stage of growth. These are parents who develop a listening stance which encourages expressions of feelings and discerns the adolescent's perspective.

2. Close, Caring Families

These families are characterized by parental harmony—demonstrating love and affection in their relationships with each other, effective parent-youth communication, consistent authoritative (democratic) parental discipline, and parental nurturing. They show affection and respect by building trust, doing things together, and developing family support systems.

3. Moral, Service-Oriented Beliefs

These parents know what their position is regarding what is right and wrong, and are able to explain the reasonableness of this position, and value discussion and exploration with their adolescents. Three parenting behaviors influence adolescent moral behavior—demonstrative affection, consistent authoritative (democratic) discipline, and inductive discussion.

4. A Personal, Liberating Faith

These parents both live and encourage their adolescent to develop a faith life that places emphasis on God's love and acceptance (liberating faith), on establishing and maintaining a close relationship to God (vertical orientation), and on reaching out and caring for others (horizontal orientation). Critical to the development of this faith is the family's faith sharing through daily interaction, structured times of worship (Sunday worship, scripture reading, celebrations, prayer time, etc.,) and works of justice and service as a family.[1]

Every parish/school can become more family-sensitive (a supportive system for family life) by offering parent programs/ services and by designing its ministries/ programs, schedules, etc., with a family perspective. In particular an adolescent catechesis program can sponsor at least three kinds of programming:

1. Programs specifically designed for parents:

a. educational experiences that communicate information on adolescent growth, develop skills for communication and for parenting;

b. parent support groups (especially for single and blend family parents and for those experiencing divorce or separation);

c. educational programs for parents on contemporary moral teachings, moral decision-making and how to communicate moral values;

d. educational programs on contemporary Church teachings.

2. Programs for parents and adolescents.

One way to integrate parents into the adolescent catechesis curriculum is to design certain courses with parent sessions that are incorporated. A course on sexuality (a great course to involve parents) might follow this sequence: a parents-only session, followed by three youth sessions, another parents-only session, then three more youth sessions, and finally a parent-teen closing session. Other possibilities for parent-teen programming include:

a. family activities and programs which build communication, trust, and closeness;

b. parent-teen programs that discuss moral values and promote discussion;

c. worship and scripture resources for parents to use in the home;

d. justice and service projects that involve the whole family (perhaps at regularly scheduled times during the year);

e. parent-teen retreat experiences; and

f. home-based advent and lenten programs (as individual families or clusters).

3. Parallel programs for adults and adolescents.

There is a critical need to develop and offer programs for parents which parallel the themes offered the young people. Parents could take an adult course (for example, morality or Scripture) while their son or daughter was participating in an adolescent course on the same topic. For many parishes/schools this is the beginning of an adult education curriculum.

---

4 **Adolescent catechesis respects the unique cultural heritages of young people and builds upon the positive values found in these cultural heritages, while at the same time engaging young people in examining their culture in the light of faith and examining their faith in the light of culture.**

We are challenged to develop a catechesis that is culturally appropriate to youth of specific ethnic cultures and to develop a multi-cultural catechesis for all youth that builds understanding and provides experiences of other cultures. Here are several guidelines that can assist you in these two tasks.

1. Know the cultures and their essential components.

Seek to understand the religious values and traditions of ethnic or racial groups that may be present in the parish or school. With this knowledge cultural variety will be welcomed as a gift to be celebrated, not as a condition to be overcome.

2. Learn their most significant expressions.

Move toward the deeper level of meaning and value. Understand the origin, meaning, and value that the group attaches to a particular ritual, prayer or belief.

3. Respect their particular values and riches.

Become aware of the limitations of your own culture so that you can appreciate the riches of other cultures. Learn from each other. Help youth sense a support for their history, culture, and religiosity. Promote liturgical and social celebrations that express the spirit and traditions of the different cultural groups present in the community, especially on occasions linked to their particular histories.[2]

Paying particular attention to the cultural foundation of catechesis (the first three guidelines) has important implications. Nathan Jones has written, "The following elements are regarded widely as foundational for religious education in black communities: a sense of self, a sense of history, a sense of community, a sense of disciplined growth, and a sense of the sacred. These elements designate key assumptions that programs typically enflesh. . . . By paying close attention to these imperatives, you can design effective programs, curricula, and select appropriate resources."[3] Each ethnic culture has these foundational elements. It is essential that adolescent catechesis builds on these foundations.

4. Respect the different learning styles of people.

Much research in the past thirty years has demonstrated that people think and learn differently, and that even different cultural groups learn in distinct ways. Two predominant styles have been identified—field independent and field sensitive or dependent. The characteristics of these two styles of learning are listed here:

Field Independent Learner:

- is usually more task oriented,
- has well developed analytical abilities.
- is motivated by individual competition and achievement,
- perceives the specific, then the totality,
- can work well alone,
- is not affected as much by outside stimuli such as the instructor or the environment when solving a problem or performing a task.

Field Sensitive or Field Dependent Learner:

- works well in groups,
- perceives the totality, then the specific,
- is motivated by group competition and achievement,
- is more affected by outside stimuli such as the instructor of the environment when solving a problem or performing a task,
- is influenced more by affective variables in learning.[4]

The particular socialization practices fostered by a cultural group and maintained in the family influences the learning styles of youth. It was found that Anglo-American learners tended to prefer a field sensitive or independent learning style, and that Hispanic-American learners tended to prefer a field dependent learning style if they were from very traditional Hispanic families. The more assimilated the Hispanic family or individual, the more he or she tended to prefer a field independent learning style.

Culture, language, religious expressions and preferred learning styles are important for a solid multicultural catechesis. The learning process, to be effective with field sensitive or dependent learners, must include deliberate strengthening of self-esteem, build a positive community learning environment, establish caring and sensitive relationships between teacher and learners, use group discussion and group activities, emphasize group cooperation and group goals, present the overall picture and lead learners to "figure it out," and utilize experiential, "hands-on," learning involving the whole person.[5]

5 Adolescent catechesis is integrated and developed within a comprehensive, multifaceted approach to ministry with youth.

We are challenged to envision and plan our catechetical efforts within a comprehensive youth ministry/high school campus ministry that includes the components outlined in the *Vision of Youth Ministry* (USCC, 1976): Evangelization, Prayer and Worship, Guidance and Healing, Community Life, Justice and Service, Enablement, and Advocacy. Catechesis is not the totality of the Church's ministry with youth, but youth ministry without catechesis is not effective youth ministry. It is within this comprehensive ministry with youth that adolescent catechesis is most effective. In order to accomplish this the adolescent catechetical curriculum must be planned and implemented within the framework of youth ministry. This calls for collaboration among leaders in ministry with youth.

Operational Principles

The following operational principles describe the principles for developing adolescent catechesis. The resources in this Manual will assist you in planning and implementing a curriculum based on these principles.

6 Adolescent catechesis responds to the developmental, social, and cultural needs of adolescence.

Related to that, the curriculum respects the changing developmental and social characteristics of the various stages of adolescence, providing a significantly different content and approach for younger and older adolescents. We are challenged to root our efforts in the lives of adolescents and to develop our catechetical efforts around the learning needs of younger adolescents (11/12-14/15 years old) and older adolescents (14/15-18/19 years old). This approach means that content (faith themes) of a curriculum will be different for younger and older adolescents. Parishes are challenged to develop a curriculum for younger adolescents and a curriculum for older adolescents based on the faith themes presented in *The Challenge.* However, simply categorizing young people into junior high and senior high will not be sufficient. Developmentally, the learning needs of many young people in the early years of high school will best be addressed through the younger adolescent faith themes. This will mean that those who are developing a high school curriculum will need to offer selected younger adolescent themes as well as the older adolescent themes.

7 Adolescent catechesis respects the variability in maturation rates and learning needs of adolescence.

We are challenged to recognize the great variability in adolescence and rethink our current system of grade levels. Using developmental and social growth as a means for planning catechesis may mean establishing one curriculum for younger adolescents and a second for older adolescents, thereby removing age-graded catechesis in parishes. This will also mean offering a variety of learning topics to respond to these varied learning needs.

8 Adolescent catechesis respects the expanding freedom and autonomy of adolescents.

We are challenged to respect the freedom of adolescents to dialogue, question, search and disagree. We are also challenged to develop catechetical programs that offer adolescents the freedom to select the topics and formats for learning.

9 Adolescent catechesis uses a variety of learning formats, environments, schedules, and educational techniques.

In light of the three preceding principles, we are challenged to develop catechetical programs with variety. No one format, environment, schedule, or educational technique will work with all adolescents. In parish settings, adolescent catechesis works best in short term, rather than long term, programming. There are a variety of learning models that can be utilized in adolescent catechesis depending on local needs, scheduling, environments, etc. Faith themes can be programmed on a weekly, bi-weekly, full day, monthly, overnight, weekend, and week-long basis, using models such as: mini-course, seasonal, peer ministry, small group, youth fellowship, intergenerational, worship/celebration, action-learning, study tour/trip, individualized learning, and learning centers.

10 **Adolescent Catechesis best responds to the learning needs of adolescents when it is focused on particular faith themes.**

This last principle challenges us to focus on selected faith themes (for example, Jesus, Morality, Sexuality, Scripture) drawn from both the Catholic Christian Tradition and the developmental and social needs of adolescents. This approach explores selected, focused content areas of a faith theme, thereby providing a more in-depth learning experience. The faith theme approach contrasts with a survey approach. A survey approach seeks to provide learners with an overview of a variety of topics related to a particular theme. While this approach is appropriate for childhood catechesis, as we seek to expose them to the scope of the Catholic Christian tradition, it is not as effective in the adolescent years. Instead of continuing the survey approach, adolescent catechesis seeks to provide the learner with focused, more in-depth learning that can be genuinely new for him or her.

In Chapter 2 we will explore the faith themes for younger and older adolescents that serve as a foundation for an adolescent catechesis curriculum.

For Further Study

Bowman, Thea. Editor. *Families—Black and Catholic, Catholic and Black.*
Washington, DC: USCC/Department of Education, 1985.

The Challenge of Adolescent Catechesis—Maturing in Faith. Washington,
DC: NFCYM Publications, 1986.

Curran, Dolores. *Traits of a Healthy Family.* Minneapolis, MN: Winston Press, 1983.

Durka. Gloria. "Family Systems: A New Perspective for Youth Ministry," in
Readings in Youth Ministry. Washington, DC: NFCYM Publications, 1986.

Faith and Culture. Washington, DC: USCC/Department of Education, 1987.

Groome, Thomas. *Christian Religious Education.* San Francisco: Harper & Row. 1981.

Herrera, Marina. "Toward Multicultural Youth Ministry," in *Readings in Youth
Ministry.* NFCYM Publications. 1986.

Hill, Brennan. "Fundamentals of Religious Education" (5-Part Series) in
PACE 17. Winona, MN: St. Mary's Press.

Jones, Nathan. *Sharing the Old, Old Story—Educational Ministry in the
Black Community.* Winona, MN: St. Mary's Press, 1982.

Shelton, Charles. *Adolescent Spirituality.* Chicago, IL: Loyola University Press, 1983.

Strommen, Merton and Irene. *Five Cries of Parents.* San Francisco: Harper & Row, 1985.

Warren, Michael. *Youth and the Future of the Church.* San Francisco: Harper & Row, 1982.

Warren, Michael, editor. *Resources in Youth Ministry.* Winona, MN: St.
Mary's Press, 1987.

Vision of Youth Ministry. Washington, DC: USCC/Department of Education, 1976.

Notes

1. Summarized from Merton and Irene Strommen, *Five Cries of Parents,*
(San Francisco, CA: Harper & Row, 1985).

2. Drawn from the article by Marina Herrera, "The Religious Education of
Hispanics in a Multicultural Church," *New Catholic World,* July/August
1980, p. 150.

3. Nathan Jones, "An Afro-American Perspective" in *Faith and Culture,*
(Washington, DC: USCC Department of Education, 1987), pp. 78-79.

4. Manuel Ramirez III and A. Casteneda, *Cultural Democracy, Bicogntive
Development and Education,* (New York: Academic Press, 1974), pp. 59- 79.

5. *Integral Education: A Response to the Hispanic Presence,* (Washington,
DC: NCEA, 1987), p.50.

2 Faith Themes for Adolescent Catechesis

No task is more important and more difficult than developing an effective and responsive adolescent catechesis curriculum. Curriculum development is grounded in the developmental, social, and cultural needs of youth *and* the wisdom of the Catholic Christian tradition. The developmental, social, and cultural research provides a guide for developing the specific content and catechetical approach for younger (11/12-14/15) and older (14/15-18/19) adolescents. In this chapter we will explore the research foundations for the faith themes for younger and older adolescents and the focus and key topics for each theme. This will serve as the basis for developing a curriculum (Chapter 3).

Integral Elements of a Curriculum

Integral to the faith themes are six elements that need to be woven throughout our teaching of each theme: **Jesus, Church, Scripture, Prayer, Action,** and **Interpretation.** We address these elements in our curriculum and in the learning plan of each faith theme by seeking to: enrich the adolescents' knowledge of and relationship with *Jesus* and the *Good News,* deepen their understanding of the *Scriptures,* promote a vision of the *Church* as an historical community committed to the vision, values and mission of Jesus, help adolescents to pray by personally and communally experiencing *prayer,* empower adolescents to *live* a more faithful Christian life, and encourage *critical reflection*

and *interpretation* of youth culture, society, and life experiences in light of the Catholic Christian Faith. Every theme in the curriculum promotes these six central elements.

Characteristics of Younger Adolescent Growth (11/12—14/15)

The characteristics of the developmental and social growth of younger adolescent, drawn from research studies, provide a basis for developing several of the faith themes for younger adolescents *and* for developing an approach to teaching each themes. Based on the research it can be said that the early adolescents undergo rapid physical, social, emotional, and intellectual changes. They change at different rates, according to highly individual "internal clocks." The following characteristics of early adolescence should be seen in a dynamic way—emerging over time, at different rates within each young person.[1]

Physical Development: Young adolescents grow more rapidly than at any other stage in their life except infancy. The three kinds of physical changes that occur are:

1. the growth spurt in height and weight;
2. the development of primary sex characteristics, the maturing of the reproductive system; and
3. the development of secondary sex characteristics, the visual signs of the maturing body, for example, body hair.

Young people at this age are sensitive about their physical changes and often are confused about their emerging sexuality. They struggle to incorporate their bodily changes into their self image. Young adolescents grow more rapidly than at any other time in their lives since birth.

Therefore: Adolescent catechesis needs to provide young adolescents with opportunities to receive accurate information and guidance about sexuality and to explore what it means to be a man or a woman and to communicate with their parents about sexuality in a Christian values-context.

Cognitive Development: Young adolescents begin to be able to think abstractly, called *formal operational thinking,* and to understand symbols and principles. They begin to reason on the basis of possibilities instead of being restricted to what they are experiencing or have experienced in the past. They develop the ability to think about their own thought—reflective thinking. Since changes in thinking ability occur gradually, it is normal for a young adolescent to think reflectively in one area but be tied to concrete thinking in another. As they work at defining themselves, they are painfully self-conscious and critical. They can sometimes become argumentative and self-centered.

Identity Development: Young adolescents are involved in a search for membership, for a sense of belonging. As they begin the process of distancing themselves from childhood, in particular as embodied in family, parental authority and parental figures, they begin to identify more strongly with the values, faith, and lifestyles of peers, heroes, or other significant adults. The values, faith and lifestyles of those who include them are the ones they most often copy or identify with. Self-identity comes from group membership for these young people. They seek limited independence and autonomy from parents and parental figures.

Therefore: Adolescent catechesis needs to provide opportunities for young adolescents to explore who they are and who they can become, to build the foundation for a strong and realistic concept of self, to reflect on their changing self-concept, to receive positive feedback on their emerging self-concept, and to experience a sense of mastery and competence.

Moral Development: Young adolescents reason morally at a conventional level—they resolve moral dilemmas in terms of the expectations of something other than themselves. This "something other" can be more personal: what their friends or other significant persons will think of them if they do or do not do such and such. It can be more impersonal: what the law or the system or good order calls for in a given situation. Loyalty and conformity to groups or rules and authority are valued highly. Acceptance and approval by others is primary.

Therefore: Adolescent catechesis needs to provide opportunities for young adolescents to gain experience in making decisions, setting rules, and shaping program content, while at the same time recognizing the limits of this freedom; to apply Christian moral values and utilize moral decision-making skills as they struggle with moral judgment questions.

Social Development: Young adolescents identify with the peer group; they want to belong, and they are developing deepening friendships. The peer group takes on new and significant importance in early adolescence. However, the parent still has a primary influence at this stage of development. It is through the peer group that the adolescent learns to develop and maintain close, supportive relationships. Social skills are often learned by trying out a variety of behaviors. Young adolescents are able to consider both parties in a relationship—the feelings, actions, and needs of those within the relationship.

Therefore: Adolescent catechesis needs to provide young adolescents with opportunities to form positive relationships and experiences with peers in a comfortable and secure environment and to develop friendship-making and friendship-maintaining skills.

Emotional Development: Dramatic body changes and difficulty in negotiating relationships with parent and peers, leaves early adolescents particularly vulnerable to bouts of low self-esteem and moodiness. Many of them deal with a high degree of pressure and stress leading some of them to act them out in ways often labeled rebellious. While this behavior is often difficult for parents and youth workers, it is important to not over-emphasize it. Early adolescence is not as stormy as much of the media suggests. It is important to distinguish between behavior that is *disturbing* or annoying to adults (for example, loud music, messy rooms) and behavior that is harmful [*disturbed*] for the young person (for example, substance abuse, depression).

Faith Development: Young adolescents seek their faith-identity in the authority of a community's understandings and ways. They are dependent upon the community for the content and shape of their faith. They need to experience the community's understandings and ways. By belonging to a Christian community they learn who they are as Christians, establishing a firm set of beliefs, attitudes and values. They want to be involved in the life and mission of the community.

At this time in their life the authority or responsibility for one's faith life is external to the self. They do not have a sure enough grasp of their own identity and autonomous judgment to construct and maintain an independent perspective. In the younger adolescent years they can begin to view their faith interpersonally, developing a personal relationship with God. God can become a personal God, who knows, accepts and confirms them deeply.

Therefore: Adolescents at this age need to experience a sense of belonging, of membership in the Christian Community and to experience the Christian Story with its understandings, rituals and actions. Adolescent catechesis needs to connect religious traditions with varied opportunities for self-discovery and self-definition and to help young people explore the religious bases of their religious faith so as to develop a religious identity rooted in the community's ways and understandings. Through this process, they can be enabled to sort out the variety of beliefs, values, and ideas that are grounded in both significant others and peer-group consensus.

Adolescent catechesis helps young people to experience Jesus from a growing inner sense of self rather than relying on external influences and to develop their relationship with Jesus—concentrating on who Jesus really is—his values, his intentions, his motives, and his attitudes as well as what he really proclaimed and how this relates to their own life. Catechesis provides young people with opportunities to discover a relationship with God in a more personal way, to reflect on the experience of God as friend or companion and what this means on an intellectual, affective, and moral level.

Adolescent catechesis needs to provide young adolescents with the opportunities to gain a sense of competence by performing meaningful tasks in their communities and in their parishes. It needs to engage young people in exploring, discussing and taking construction action on justice and peace concerns.

In addition, adolescent catechesis needs to provide younger adolescents with opportunities to develop relationships with diverse adult, Catholic Christian role models and skills for communicating with adults and to experience mature adults who are comfortable with them and are willing to explore sensitive issues with them. Adults who will share their own life experiences that relay themes of personal relating and personal commitment.

Faith Themes for Younger Adolescent Catechesis

Building on the developmental and social research, *The Challenge* recommends the following faith themes as the foundation for a curriculum for youth aged 11/12-14/15. The focus of these faith themes reflects the changes that younger adolescents are experiencing. Many themes engage the younger adolescent in exploring how the Christian faith responds to these changes (for example, Personal Growth, Relationships, Sexuality). Other themes offer a new perspective on the early adolescent's faith (for example, Jesus, Moral Decision-Making).

If you are developing a program for your junior high school youth, then these themes will form the basis for your curriculum. If you are developing a curriculum for high school youth, then several of the younger adolescent faith themes will need to be offered with the older adolescent faith themes. Here is a summary of the focus for each faith theme. (Consult *The Challenge* for more detailed information on the faith themes.)

Church—understanding and experiencing the Church's story, mission and ministries, and becoming involved in the life and work of the community.

Jesus and the Gospel Message—developing a more personal relationship with Jesus, learning what it means to be a disciple of Jesus as a younger adolescent, learning about the life, mission and teaching of Jesus.

Moral Decision-Making—learning how to make moral decisions based on the Catholic Christian moral norms as younger adolescents face increasingly more complex moral decisions and dilemmas.

Personal Growth—developing a stronger and more realistic concept of self by exploring who they are and who they can become as Christians; exploring Jesus' vision of being fully human; learning how the Good News addresses adolescent struggles and problems.

Relationships—learning how to develop honest, loving, respectful and trusting relationships with peers, parents, and other adults; learning how to make and maintain relationships; exploring the scriptural teaching on relationships.

Service—exploring Jesus' call to live a life of loving service that is integral to discipleship, developing a foundation for a social justice consciousness, and participating in service/action for justice.

Human Sexuality—learning about sexual development, relationships and dating, and the dynamics of maturing as a sexual person within a family and Catholic Christian's value context; exploring Catholic sexual moral values.

Characteristics of Older Adolescent Growth (14/15—18/19)[2]

Cognitive Development: Older adolescents are capable of moving toward critical consciousness—the ability to think about their thinking, to be conscious and critical of their own consciousness. This second level of reflection (not only "what do I think" but also "why do I think that") makes it possible for them to grow toward a personal identity, moral value system, personal faith identity.

Identity Development: The establishment of a personal identity is the central task of older adolescence. Older adolescents seek to develop a commitment to a personally-held system of values, religious beliefs, vocational goals, and philosophy of life. The search for an identity involves the establishment of a meaningful self-concept in which past, present, and future are brought together to from a unified whole. They must answer, for themselves, the questions: "Who am I?" and "Who am I to become?" The process of identity achievement also brings with it questioning, reevaluation, and experimentation. Older adolescents develop further autonomy from parents, an autonomy that involves independence of action. They work to accept their sexuality and conceptualize a sex-role identity (self-definition as a man or woman) that will continue through young adulthood and into middle adulthood. They are engaged in making decisions regarding career choice and often experiment with one or more careers before deciding on an "adult" career.

Therefore: Adolescent catechesis needs to provide older adolescents with the opportunities to explore their sexuality and their sex-role identity in a Christian value-based approach; to develop the decision-making skills needed to confront adult life decisions, for example, career and lifestyle; to reach outward toward future Christian adulthood.

29

In this process, the need for relationships, an occupational role, and a value system is integral for identity achievement. The call of the gospel resonates with the emerging identity to foster faith growth that accepts the adolescent, and yet challenges the person to future growth.

Moral Development: Older adolescents exercise moral judgments in matters of much greater complexity. They are beginning to develop an internalized morality, a mature value system that can guide their behavior. In this process they are searching for a moral code which preserves their personal integrity.

Many older adolescents continue to reason morally at a conventional level, that is, they resolve moral dilemmas in terms of the expectations of something other than themselves, personal or impersonal. Others move beyond conventional moral reasoning, evaluating earlier (inherited) moral principles in light of new experience and information. Many older adolescents may appear skeptical, negative, and relativistic because of this evaluation process. Gradually, many older adolescents begin developing a principled, more personal form of moral reasoning. They come to realize that to be true to oneself one must act upon the moral principles to which one is committed. They come to recognize moral principles that are followed for their own sake, for example, justice, love and care, equality, etc. Right and wrong are determined according to these universal principles.

Therefore: Adolescent catechesis needs to provide older adolescents with the opportunities to foster a reflective critique of their personal and social values, enabling them to develop a personal, comprehensive, and more principled Christian value system. The goal is to assist older adolescents in developing an interiorized moral value system using a principled, more personal form of moral reasoning. Understanding the role of Christian conscience and moral decision-making will be critical to the development of an interiorized moral value system.

Development of Intimacy: Older adolescents develop deep, trusting, enduring personal friendships—with members of the same sex and members of opposite sex. In older adolescence relationships become mutual and intimate. They look for acceptance and love—to be "who I am" and to be really accepted by others; to be able to share honestly their deepest selves with another.

Interpersonal Development: Older adolescents begin the process of expanding their perspective to encompass self, peer group, and the larger world or society. The attitudes and views of the larger world are increasingly understood and taken into consideration. They can comprehend more deeply the motives, feelings, and thought patterns of other individuals and groups of peoples, such as nations and classes. They realize that other individuals are acting out of beliefs, attitudes, and values that may differ from their own belief system.

Therefore: Adolescent catechesis needs to provide older adolescents with the opportunities to develop a social consciousness perspective that is attentive to the needs of those who are suffering and being oppressed in our world. Broader social reasoning means a widening understanding of others which permits the older adolescent to appreciate others and to care more deeply. Older adolescents are capable of developing a global perspective and thinking and acting concertedly for justice and peace at the personal, interpersonal, and social structural levels of their lives.

Faith Development: Many older adolescents begin to reflect critically on the meaning of their own life and faith. They search for the foundations of a faith life that will provide them with meaning. They begin to take responsibility for their own faith life and journey. Critical judgment of the community's understandings and ways emerge as they strive to discover convictions worth living for. In this process these seek to establish their own faith identity, a faith life that is personally held and valued. They take seriously the burden of responsibility for their own commitments, lifestyles, beliefs and attitudes. They are developing an inner-directed faith identity. They are concerned with the integrity of belief and action.

Therefore: Adolescent catechesis needs to provide older adolescents with the opportunities to explore what it means to be a Christian, a Catholic, a person of faith, and an individual who holds distinct, personal views. In this time of exploring their faith, it is critical that older adolescents reflect on their faith life, critically appraise the faith of the community so as to establish their own personally-held faith system. It is helpful to explore with the older adolescent questions concerning commitment (What types of commitment?), values (What is important in my life?) and beliefs (What do I believe?). Increasing attention should be paid to helping the older adolescents take personal responsibility for their faith life.

Adolescent catechesis also needs to provide older adolescents with the opportunities to develop a personal, deeply relational experience of Jesus Christ—that is enhanced by their need for achieving a personal identity and establishing intimacy. Some of the deepest experiences in any human being arise from the development of intimate relationships. These relational experiences express what being a Christian means, namely, the sharing of myself based on the life, death, and resurrection of Jesus. Thus, attention to this relational sphere of adolescent growth is critically important because relationships mirror both a personal experience of God's love and a conscious presence of this love in the young person's life.

Adolescent catechesis also needs to provide older adolescents with the opportunities to develop a personal spirituality and a rich personal prayer life. The process of developing a personal faith identity and the qualities of intimacy in relationships prepares older adolescents for the development of a personal spirituality and prayer life. By experiencing variety of approaches to prayer and the spiritual life, adolescents can forge a personal spirituality and a lifelong pattern of prayer.

Lastly, older adolescents need to develop relationships with adult Catholic Christians who will affirm their struggle, listen to their stories and questions, share their own faith journey, and ask questions that encourage critical thinking and reflection.

Faith Themes for Older Adolescent Catechesis

Building on developmental and social research, *The Challenge* recommends the following faith themes as the foundation for a curriculum for youth aged 14/15—18/19. The focus of these faith themes reflects the future that older adolescents will be facing. These faith themes provide older adolescents with a faith direction toward the future. Many themes engage older adolescents in exploring how the Christian faith responds to their developing identity and future life (Jesus, Justice, Love and Lifestyles, Faith and Identity, Morality, and Prayer and Worship/ Spirituality). Other themes offer new understandings and skills essential for an adult Christian's life (learning how to read and interpret the Gospels, Hebrew Scriptures, and Paul and His Letters). Here is a summary of the focus for each faith theme. (Consult *The Challenge* for more detailed information on the faith themes.)

Faith and Identity—exploring what Christian faith is and what it means to be a faithful person; exploring the core beliefs of the Catholic Church; developing a personally-held Catholic faith which is integral to one's growing identity.

The Gospels—understanding the historical and literary development, structure, and major themes of the four gospels; learning to how to read and interpret the gospels.

Hebrew Scriptures—understanding the historical and literary development, structure, and major themes of the Hebrew Scriptures; learning how to interpret and read the Hebrew Scriptures.

Jesus—exploring Jesus the Christ of the Gospels (life, mission, key teachings, death and resurrection) and of history; discovering the meaning of Jesus for today; developing a more deeply relational experience of Jesus.

Justice and Peace—developing a justice spirituality by exploring the Hebrew Scriptures, Jesus' teachings, and contemporary Catholic social teachings; developing a global awareness of justice and peace by learning how to analyze social issues; learning how to act on behalf of justice and peace—personally, interpersonally, and socially (local, national and global).

Love and Lifestyles—exploring the Catholic view of sexuality and intimacy; learning how to build love relationships and intimacy; exploring Christian marriage and family; learning life decision-making skills.

Morality—developing an interiorized, principled Catholic moral value system; understanding the role of Christian conscience and how to make moral decisions as a Christian, learning how to reflect critically on the values of society and culture in light of Catholic moral norms.

Paul and His Letters—understanding the historical context, literary style and major themes of Paul's letters; learning to interpret his writings; and exploring Paul as apostle, preacher, theologian, and man of faith.

Prayer and Worship—developing a spirituality for one's adult life; exploring the Catholic tradition of prayer and worship; learning how to pray—personally and communally.

For Further Study

Elkind, David. *All Grown Up and No Place to Go.* Reading, MA: Addisson-Wesley. 1984.

Farel, Anita. *Early Adolescence and Religion.* Carrboro, NC: Center for Early Adolescence. 1982.

Fowler, James. *Stages of Faith.* San Francisco: Harper & Row. 1981.

Groome, Thomas. "On Being 'With' Late Adolescents in Ministry," in *Readings in Youth Ministry.* Washington, DC: NFCYM Publications. 1986.

Nelson, John S. "Research on Adolescent Moral and Faith Development," in *Readings in Youth Ministry.* Washington, DC: NFCYM Publications. 1986.

Parks, Sharon. *The Critical Years—The Young Adult Search for a Faith to Live By.* San Francisco: Harper & Row. 1986.

Shelton, Charles. *Adolescent Spirituality.* Chicago: Loyola University Press. 1983.

Notes

1. To develop this profile the following sources were used:

   Anita Farel. *Early Adolescence and Religion.* (Carrboro, NC: Center for Early Adolescence, 1982).

   Readings in Youth Ministry. (Washington, DC: NFCYM Publications, 1986).

   Charles Shelton. *Adolescent Spirituality.* Chicago: Loyola University Press, 1983.

2. To develop this profile the following sources were used:

   James Fowler. *Stages of Faith.* (San Francisco: Harper & Row, 1981).

   Readings in Youth Ministry. (Washington, DC: NFCYM Publications, 1986).

   Charles Shelton. *Adolescent Spirituality.* (Chicago: Loyola University Press, 1983).

Chapter **3** Designing an Adolescent Catechetical Curriculum

Introduction

There are several key principles that guide the process of curriculum development. *First,* this process relies on gathering a *Team* of curriculum planners who are committed to planning. This team should include the key leaders who are responsible for adolescent catechesis in your setting. A suggested list of team members in a parish would include the Coordinator of Youth Ministry, Director of Religious Education, catechists, adult leaders, parents, and youth leaders. A suggested list of team members in a school might include the Religion Department Chairperson, Campus Minister/Chaplain, religion teachers, principal or administrative representative, parents, and

youth representatives. Usually 12-15 people is a maximum number for a team.

Second, the process of planning is as important as the product. The team approach to planning emphasizes collaboration and shared decision-making which builds a strong sense of *ownership* among team members. This ownership extends the responsibility for catechesis beyond the coordinators and catechists/religion teachers to the community-at-large. *Third,* planners need to pray for guidance, courage, creativity, and obedience to the Spirit in their decision-making. Curriculum planning needs to be a reflective, prayerful experience.

Overview of the Process

Step 1 Education on *The Challenge of Adolescent Catechesis*

Step 2 Listening to the learners: needs assessment

Step 3 Determining the faith themes

Step 4 Developing a curriculum model

Step 5 Designing the learning plan for each faith theme

Step 6 Developing an overall curriculum and calendar

Step 7 Developing leaders for adolescent catechesis

Step 8 Enrolling the participants

Step 9 Evaluating the curriculum

The Process

Step 1

Education on *The Challenge of Adolescent Catechesis*

To introduce the curriculum planners to the vision of adolescent catechesis developed in *The Challenge,* the following workshop design is recommended. This first step combines study with an evaluation of current efforts in light of *The Challenge.* Allow 2-2$\frac{1}{2}$ hours for this first meeting. [Every member of your team should have a copy of *The Challenge of Adolescent Catechesis.* To purchase it, write: NFCYM, 3900-A Harewood Rd., NE, Washington, DC 20017.]

1. **Vision of Youth Ministry and Adolescent Catechesis** (15 minutes)

   Using the material offered in the Introduction and Chapter 1 of this Manual, present the broader ministerial context for adolescent catechesis, the role of catechesis within youth ministry, and the foundations of *The Challenge.*

   ### Resources

   The Challenge of Adolescent Catechesis Vision of Youth Ministry (Department of Education, USCC) 1976.

2. **The Aim of Adolescent Catechesis** (30 minutes)

   a. *Individual Reflection* (5 minutes)
   - What do you hope will be accomplished in the lives of youth through adolescent catechesis?
   - For you, what are the goal(s) of adolescent catechesis?

   b. *Sharing* (10 minutes)
   Ask the participants to share their responses to the questions.

   c. *Presentation and Discussion* (15 minutes)
   Present the definition of adolescent catechesis as found in Chapter 1 of this Manual or on page 4 in *The Challenge.* Using Chapter 1 of this Manual or Part III

of *The Challenge* (page 8), review the aims of adolescent catechesis and the characteristics of adolescent maturing. Be sure to connect your presentation to the responses shared above. Invite questions after your presentation. After your presentation ask the participants to reflect on how they were affirmed by your presentation and how they were challenged by it. [I was affirmed by . . . ; I was challenged by . . .]

3. **Principles of Adolescent Catechesis** (50 minutes)

   a. *Presentation* (10 minutes)
   Describe the five foundational principles of adolescent catechesis using the presentation in Chapter 1 of this Manual. Give concrete examples of the implications of these principles for adolescent catechesis.

   b. *Reflection* (5 minutes)
   Using *Worksheet #1,* ask each person to assess how the five foundational principles are embodied in her or his ministry (courses, retreats).

   c. *Profile* (10 minutes)
   Take the principles, one at a time, and ask each participant to share how they see the principles embodied in her or his ministry, and whether it is operating effectively or not. Develop a profile for each principle using the responses to each of the questions. Record this information on newsprint.

   d. *Presentation* (10 minutes)
   Describe the five operational principles of adolescent catechesis using Chapter 1 of this Manual. Give concrete examples for each of these principles.

   e. *Reflection* (5 minutes)
   Using *Worksheet #2,* ask each person to assess how the five operational principles are implemented in your catechetical programs and the obstacles to implementation.

f. *Profile* (10 minutes)
Take the principles, one at a time, and ask each participant to share what is helping the implementation of the principle and what are the obstacles that hinder implementation. Develop a profile for each principle using the responses to each of the questions. Record this information on newsprint.

4. Faith Themes for Adolescent Catechesis (40 minutes)

a. *Presentation* (20 minutes)
Using the description of the faith themes in Chapter 2 of this Manual or in Part IV of *The Challenge,* present the focus and suggested content of each theme for younger and older adolescents. Compare the different content and approach between younger and older adolescent themes by using the Jesus or Morality or Service-Justice themes. Present the psychological and social background for the development of the faith themes using the material in Chapter 2 of this Manual.

b. *Reflection* (10 minutes)
Using *Worksheet #3,* ask each person (or the team, in general) to assess how the current catechetical curriculum embodies the faith themes.

c. *Profile* (10 minutes)
Take the faith themes, one at a time, and develop a profile of how each faith theme is or is not being covered in the curriculum. Record this information on newsprint. This profile can become the basis for improving a catechetical program.

5. Summary

This workshop will build a data base of needs that you address in curriculum planning. Be sure to keep the reports of each step in the workshop.

Step 2

Listening to the Learners: Needs Assessment

An assessment of the learning needs of youth will help to develop the priorities for learning in your local setting. A needs assessment also builds ownership and interest in the young people when they see programs offered are in response to their expressed needs and interests. Needs Assessment Tools #1, #2, and #3, included at the end of this chapter, use the faith themes from *The Challenge* and translates them into a format in which young people can indicate their interest and/or concerns regarding that theme. Feel free to revise and adapt these tools for your own situation.

To determine the learning needs of the young people, you can use Phone Interviews, Surveys/ Interest Finders or Youth Hearings. Samples are found at the end of this chapter. If you select the *interview* approach, design a standard instrument that each interviewer can use. For example, you can take the *Topical Ranking Survey* and ask each young person to select the five topics they would most like to explore. If you select the *survey* approach, distribute the survey where people are gathered (e.g. after the Sunday masses, at youth programs, etc.). Be sure to survey parents of youth as well. You can determine their own interest in parent programming as well as their expectations for the adolescent catechesis curriculum. If you select the *youth hearings* approach, be sure to advertise very well and offer an enticement to participate (like a dance afterwards, social activity, party, refreshments, etc.). In all three techniques, be sure to include a way for the young people to indicate what age they are so that you can group learning needs into younger and older adolescence.

Once you have compiled the results of your needs assessment, prioritize the top learning needs of younger and older adolescents. This prioritized list will give you a good indication of the starting point for your curriculum offerings or the basis of changing your current curriculum.

To tabulate the *Youth Survey,* first divide the surveys into grade level categories. Then, take the surveys and add the "3" and "4" responses (high interest). After you have finished all the surveys in your grade category, prioritize the interest items starting with the item that receives the highest number of "3" and "4" responses. Use the grade categories to develop a profile of each grade in your program. Using the faith themes for younger and older adolescents as a guide, determine which need relates to which faith theme. In this way you can determine the priorities of younger adolescents and older adolescents. If you are planning a high school curriculum, remember that high school students may need themes taken from both the younger adolescent and older adolescent faith themes. Lastly, tabulate the best times and frequency for participation by adding the checks for each of the items.

To tabulate the *Parent Survey,* take "Section A" and add the "3" and "4" responses (high interest). After you have finished tabulating all the Section A for all the surveys, prioritize the interest items starting with the item that receives the highest number of "3" and "4" responses. Then take "Section B" and record the number of responses for V, I, and U. Add the total number of responses for V, I, and U for each question.

To tabulate the *Topical Ranking Survey,* give each response a weighting (each #1 receives 1 vote; each #15 receives 15 votes), then add up the number ranking given by the young people. You now have a score for each item. Prioritize the items starting with the lowest total score (which is your highest priority) and moving to the highest score (which is your lowest priority). Use the age or grade breakdown to develop a profile of each age or grade in your program. In this way you can determine the priorities of the younger adolescent and older adolescent programs. If you are planning a high school curriculum remember that high school students may need themes taken from both the younger and older adolescent faith themes. Using the faith themes for younger and older adolescents as a guide determine which topics will become part of the high school curriculum. Lastly, tabulate the best times and frequency for participation by adding the checks for each of the items.

Determining the Faith Themes

The third step in designing an adolescent catechetical curriculum is to determine which faith themes you will be offering. In order to do this you should have evaluated the current curriculum and prioritized the key learning needs which surfaced from your needs assessment. With this data you now have a series of important recommendations that need to influence your faith theme planning.

Review the faith themes presented in Chapter 2 of this Manual or from Part IV in *The Challenge.* Then ask each person to select the priority faith themes for your curriculum, distinguishing the younger adolescent themes from the older adolescent themes. Be sure to remind the participants to consider all sources of data: *The Challenge;* the evaluation results from Worksheets #1, 2, and 3; and the needs assessment results. After each person has individually prioritized the themes, record the choices and tally the results. Using a consensus model of decision-making, select the faith themes for your younger adolescent and older adolescent curriculum. Now you are ready to organize your priority themes into a curriculum model with a particular time frame selection.

Developing a Curriculum Model

Curriculum models provide an overall schema for organizing the faith themes. Deciding (or creating) your curriculum model will greatly assist you in designing a learning plan for each faith theme (Step 5). Several curriculum models are outlined in Chapter 4 of this Manual. You may find it best to create your own curriculum model by adapting or blending these models.

It is important to apply the principles of adolescent catechesis from *The Challenge* in developing your curriculum model (see Chapter 1 of this manual or Part III in *The Challenge*).

You can recognize the great variability in adolescence by developing non-graded approaches *(Principle #7)*. Using developmental and social growth as means for planning catechesis, it might mean establishing one curriculum for younger adolescents and a second for older adolescents. This will also mean offering a variety of learning topics to respond to their varied learning needs. We can develop catechetical programs that offer adolescents the freedom to select the topics and formats for learning *(Principle #8)*. We can develop catechetical programs with variety in format, environment, schedule, and educational technique *(Principle #9)*. We can develop courses based around faith themes drawn from both the Catholic Christian Tradition and the developmental and social needs of adolescents as outlined in *The Challenge (Principle #10)*.

Consider the following questions, based on the principles of adolescent catechesis, in evaluating models or in developing your model:

- Does your model demonstrate a commitment to lifelong catechesis?
- Does your model support, encourage, and involve parents/families?
- Does your model demonstrate a respect for the cultural heritages of your youth?
- Is your model integrated into the total parish or school ministry with youth? (See *Vision of Youth Ministry.* USCC, Department of Education, 1976.)
- Does your model respond, in practice, to the developmental, social, cultural needs of adolescents?
- Does your model respect the variability in maturation and learning needs of adolescents? If your model uses age-grading, how will you account for the variability in maturation and learning needs?
- Does your model respect the expanding freedom and autonomy of adolescents? Does your model allow youth freedom to choose the faith themes that best respond to their learning needs?
- Does your model allow for a variety of learning formats, environments, schedules, and educational techniques?

Designing the Learning Plan for Each Faith Theme

Now that you have selected or created your curriculum model, you are ready to select the time frame for the curriculum. For schools this may mean choosing to develop a four-year curriculum or a two-year younger adolescent curriculum and a two-year older adolescent curriculum. In addition, it is important to decide if courses are designed on a full year, semester, or quarterly basis or if there is flexibility in determining length. Parishes can choose to develop a younger and older adolescent curriculum, and to organize program offerings on a four-month or seasonal time frame with selected themes in each season or on a full year basis or on a multi-year basis.

Seasonal Approach

If the seasonal or four-month time frame is adopted, the needs assessments will help you determine the priority faith themes for the first season. You will have to limit your offerings based on the number of young people and number of catechists. At the end of the season the curriculum is evaluated and the design for the next season determined. In the second season, you can repeat several priority faith themes while offering new faith themes from your needs assessment. Each season continues the practice of continuing some themes while adding new ones. Over the course of several seasons a pattern or sequence may evolve. Remember that it is important to offer all of the younger and older adolescent faith themes throughout a two-three year sequence. For those planning a curriculum for the first time, the seasonal approach is an easier place to begin.

Full Year and Multi-Year Approaches

A second approach is to design the entire year's curriculum, scheduling the faith themes throughout the year on a semester or quarterly basis. The priority faith themes for younger and older adolescence, as determined by your needs assessment, can serve as the basis for the curriculum.

Both the full year approach and seasonal approach can be developed into an integrated multi-year curriculum. You can build a multi-year curriculum through several years of actual programming or develop the entire program from the start and continually evaluate its effectiveness.

Now that you have determined the faith themes for younger and older adolescence, the curriculum model, and the time frame, you are ready to design the specific learning plan for each faith theme. You can divide your planning team into subgroups to plan each of the themes. The following outline shows how to develop a learning plan. [Included at the end of section are two examples of completed learning plans and a form you can reproduce to develop your own learning plans.] There are nine elements in designing a learning plan for a faith theme:

1. Determining the faith theme;

2. Developing a focus for the learning plan;

3. Developing topics;

4. Developing learning objectives;

5. Choosing learning models;

6. Selecting the setting, dates and times;

7. Locating resources/materials;

8. Determining the leaders that are required for implementing the learning plan, and

9. Determining who will design the learning experience.

Designing a Faith Theme Learning Plan

Faith Theme

Identify your theme and develop a working title.

Focus

This is a statement of two or three sentences or phrases describing the central emphasis of the learning plan. This can be adapted directly from the description of the faith themes in *The Challenge of Adolescent Catechesis.* Be sure to specify younger or older adolescence.

Developing Learning Topics

Topics are the specific issues, questions, and concepts with which the faith theme will be concerned. Topics are developed by exploring the needs of the youth and of the faith theme (see suggested content for each faith theme in *The Challenge*) and putting them into questions or statements that the learners will explore. This is the statement of the content of this learning plan. Consult the teaching resources on your faith theme for assistance in developing topics.

Developing Learning Objectives

Learning objectives state the hoped-for outcomes of the session, written in terms of what the learner will be able to do. Using the understanding of faith as trusting, believing, and doing presented in *The Challenge,* develop learning objectives for each of these activities of faith: Trusting (affective), Believing (cognitive), and Doing (lifestyle/behavioral). [See Chapter 1 in this Manual, and "Rooted in Christian Faith" on page 5 in *The Challenge*]. If adolescent catechesis is to embody this comprehensive understanding of faith, it must be built into the learning objectives for each faith theme learning plan.

To develop objectives complete the following sentence. At the conclusion of this faith theme the learner should be open to:

Trusting (*Affective*): _____

_____

Believing (*Cognitive*): _____

_____

Doing (*Lifestyle/Behavioral*): _____

_____

Choosing Learning Models

There are a variety of learning models that can be used in an adolescent catechetical curriculum. It is highly recommended that your curriculum contain a variety of learning models. It is important to select learning models which will be most effective in helping you reach your learning objectives. Certain models will be more appropriate for parishes than schools, for younger adolescents than older adolescents. [See Chapter 5 of this Manual for various models.]

Selecting the Setting, Dates, Times

While many decisions regarding setting and scheduling of dates and times are already made in a school context, flexibility is still possible. Parishes, on the other hand, have a whole set of decisions that need to be made. The following is a guide to selecting the setting, dates, and times.

First, regarding the *schedule.* Exactly how many sessions will there be? What are the dates? What is the beginning and closing time for each session? Will there be any special events with a different schedule? Have all these dates and times been entered on the church calendar, and youth ministry calendar? Who will do that? Are there any conflicts? Are there other events in the church or community that might be related to your faith theme?

Second, regarding the *setting* or place. The setting for catechesis can help or hinder the learning experience. The setting both limits and expands the learning opportunities for the young people. It is important to select a setting only after evaluating its contribution to the learning experience and how it limits and expands the learning opportunity. The church building, school, homes, retreat centers, parish, camp grounds, conference centers are just some of the locations that are possible.

Here is a quick checklist of features you may be looking for in the ideal location for your learning experience. Which of these are necessary for you?

— Enough space for activities?
— Flexible?
— Attractive, colorful?
— Good light?
— Good ventilation?
— Free of interruption?
— Won't disturb others?
— Carpet?
— Comfortable chairs?
— Restrooms nearby?
— Walls for display?
— A-V's can be used?
— Refreshments can be served?
— Available when you need it?

Remember that we also learn from our environment. A dingy, messy, crowded room is teaching everyone present something about church An entirely bare room, three times too large for the group, teaches something else. Choose your setting with care, and help to prepare it for the best possible learning experience.

Locating Resources/Materials

What print and audio-visual materials are available for you to use in designing the learning program? Appropriate audio-visual resources are often listed in the leader guide to youth booklets. Consult your diocesan media resource center, regional centers, university resource centers for audio-visual resources. Another source of materials are catalogs from religious education publishers and film libraries and producers.

Leaders Required

Who will be needed to conduct the learning program? A course may need only one catechist, while a weekend learning program may need catechists, resource people, group leaders, prayer coordinator, *et al.* Determining what needs to be done (leader tasks) and what leadership jobs are needed is the first step in finding leaders. [Consult Step 7—Developing Leaders for Adolescent Catechesis—for assistance in recruiting, training, and support leaders.]

Learning Experience Designers

Who will be involved in designing the actual learning experiences? Will the catechist work alone or will a team be involved in designing? Who will provide guidance and resources for the learning experience designers? Often times the coordinator (D.R.E., Youth Minister, Religion Department Chairperson) is involved in designing the learning experience with the catechist/religion teacher.

Developing an Overall Curriculum and Calendar

Using your curriculum model, take all your individual learning plans and weave them into an overall curriculum plan. You have now constructed your curriculum for one season, one year, or for your entire younger or older adolescent program. If you chose the seasonal approach, planning for the next season will mean evaluating the first season and adding or revising learning plans.

Now evaluate your curriculum, using the following questions:

- Does your curriculum demonstrate a commitment to lifelong catechesis?
- Does your curriculum support, encourage, and involve parents/families?
- Does your curriculum demonstrate a respect for the cultural heritages of your youth?
- Is your curriculum integrated into the total parish or school ministry with youth?.(See *Vision of Youth Ministry.* USCC, Department of Education, 1976.)
- Does your curriculum respond, in practice, to the developmental, social, cultural needs of adolescents?
- Does your curriculum respect the variability in maturation and learning needs of adolescents? If your model uses age-grading, how will you account for the variability in maturation and learning needs?
- Does your curriculum respect the expanding freedom and autonomy of adolescents? Does your model allow youth freedom to choose the faith themes that best respond to their learning needs?
- Does your curriculum allow for a variety of learning formats, environments, schedules, and educational techniques?

Second, develop a calendar to schedule all the learning plans. Be sure to integrate your curriculum into the overall youth ministry (parish or school) for the coming year. Inevitably, you will have some scheduling and/or setting conflicts.

Developing Leaders for Adolescent Catechesis

Now that the curriculum is designed, leadership development becomes a priority: recruiting, training, and supporting catechetical leaders. A brief overview of leader development is provided below. This process is designed primarily for parish use, but may be helpful on specific school projects which require leaders (for example, retreats, liturgy planning) [For a detailed description of these steps refer to: *Leadership for Youth Ministry.* Fox, Guerin, Reynolds, and Roberto. (Winona, MN: St. Mary's Press, 1984).]

Overview

1. **Develop Leadership Positions**

   a. Describe the programs for which leaders will be needed.
   b. List tasks which leader will perform in each program.
   c. List positions for which leaders will be needed.
   d. Write job descriptions for each leadership position.

2. **Recruit Leaders**

   a. Search for persons with leadership potential.
   b. Invite prospects to serve.
   c. Place leaders in leadership positions.

3. **Education of Leaders**

   a. Orient new leaders.
   b. Diagnose the learning needs of the leaders.
   c. Location, plan, and provide opportunities for learning.

4. **Support Leaders**

   a. Authorize leaders to begin service.
   b. Engage leaders in support-guidance groups.
   c. Provide the information and resources which leaders need.
   d. Express and celebrate the support of the parish or school.

The Process

This approach to developing a leadership system begins with the leadership needs of your programs and then moves to recruit people to fill those leadership positions. Many efforts at recruiting leaders fail because the leadership jobs are not clearly defined. Central to this leadership system is the development of clear job descriptions which are used as the basis of recruiting leaders. Here is brief description of each of the four steps.

1. Develop Leadership Positions

Begin your work by describing the programs for which leaders will be needed. For each program, list the tasks which leaders will perform. Be very specific. Often times we assume that our leaders know what tasks are involving in planning or conducting a specific program. We need to identify clearly the tasks that are involved in conducting a program. Once you have listed the necessary tasks, group these tasks in a series of leadership positions. It is better to identify many leadership positions with fewer tasks than to identify one or two positions with a large number of tasks. You can always group leadership positions together. It is much easier to recruit several leaders for smaller jobs than to find one person to take on a large job. Now that you have identified leadership positions, develop job descriptions for each leadership position. Even though developing job descriptions takes time, it will serve as the basis for recruiting, training, supporting, and evaluating your leaders. [At the end of this chapter there are sample worksheets to define leadership positions and to develop job descriptions. Also included is a sample job description for a catechist.]

2. Recruit Leaders

Now that you have identified the leadership positions you need to fill and the requirements of each job, you are ready to develop your recruitment plan. The first thing that needs to be said about recruitment is

that it is a year-round task. The first element in the recruitment process is general recruitment. This involves sharing with the entire community the leadership needs of the youth ministry. This can be done through the parish newsletter and/or bulletin, brochures, displays and posters, presentations to groups, and a time-and-talent survey. If you use the bulletin/newsletter or a brochure, translate your job descriptions into brief want-ads. In your brochure you can include an application that prospective leaders can fill out. Using the want-ad approach gets away from "pleading" or "begging" for volunteers. Usually the latter approach does not attract the best people, and consequently, you are faced with "de-volunteering" a leader. Develop an approach that spells out what is required. This will usually self-select the right people. Another form of general recruitment is to ask the staff and key leaders in the community for their recommendations. Be sure to ask the young people also. Develop a file on each prospective leader. [At the end of this chapter there is a sample application form that you can use with your brochure and time-and-talent survey.]

Follow up your general recruitment with interviews of all prospective leaders. Through your interviews you can determine if they are right for the job or if you should recommend another job. Only after someone has been interviewed should the person be confirmed as a leader. At your interview you will be able to determine if the person is ready to serve or needs training or needs to explore the job first before he or she decides. Often times it helps to set up interview teams (an adult and young person). This helps share the responsibility for interviewing.

3. Education of Leaders

Education of leaders involves three major elements: orienting new leaders; diagnosing the learning needs of your leaders; and providing pre-service, in-service, and continuing education opportunities. A key to developing the education component of your leader system is that you do not have to conduct the training yourself. It *is* your responsibility to locate or provide the training opportunities for your leaders.

First, all new leaders need an orientation to adolescent catechesis and youth ministry, to your community's programming, and to their job. This is an opportunity to build community among your leaders and to show them how their particular job fits into the broader ministry with youth. Second, you will need to diagnose their learning needs. Your training opportunities are developed around these learning needs. This means that you can personalize the training. Not everyone requires the same training for his or her particular job. Remember that many leaders have experience and abilities that you can build on. Third, locate, plan, and provide opportunities for training. In order to do this you will need to become familiar with all the possibilities within your parish/congregation, diocese/synod, colleges, or community agencies. Also become aware of the audio and video resources that can be used to train your leaders. [Note: The educational designs offered in the *Enablement Resource Manual* can be used to develop an orientation program and a catechist education program.]

4. Support Leaders

The first three steps in developing your leadership system result in placing leaders in leadership positions. Now you want to keep them. Supporting your leaders is a year-round task. Leaders need to be authorized to begin their service. Such authorization or commissioning should be done in a public way to recognize the ministry of these leaders. Second, establish support-guidance groups for your leaders and then schedule them into your calendar. Try not to involve your leaders in any programming during the weeks in which you meet in support-guidance groups. These meetings provide an opportunity to build community, resource your leaders, share joys and struggles, and

support each other, especially through prayer. Third, provide the information and resources which your leaders need for their work. The establishment of a library/resource center is a must. Lastly, if you want to keep your leaders thank them regularly through gatherings, Christmas gift (a book or subscription to a magazine that will help them in their ministry), and a yearly banquet or celebration to express and celebrate the support of the church.

Inviting the Participants

In parishes, a special letter or invitation with a brochure can be sent to every young person announcing the program. This special targeted mailing is personal and relational. A letter and brochure targeted directly to parents also includes them in the year's program and asks them to encourage (not force) their son's or daughter's participation. In addition to written invitations, phone calls can be made to each young person inviting them to participate.

Step 8

Enrolling the Participants

Enrolling participants is the final step in your curriculum design prior to implementing the curriculum. Many of these four procedures may be done as part of the overall promotion of the youth ministry programming (parish) or course offerings (school) for the coming year. If that is done, be sure to include your specific programming. If not, you will probably need to engage in the following three tasks.

Promoting the Program

Plan for general promotion of the program to the entire parish community as well as the young people. Special brochures with the calendar of the season or year, bulletin announcements each week, a newsletter or posters are all ways to get the news to people. Be sure to start early! In a school, if you are developing a curriculum with electives or options, a special brochure describing the courses and programs would be an excellent way to communicate the new curriculum. If you use a brochure, be sure to include a sign-up sheet for youth to register their selections.

Registering Participants

A good technique for enhancing participant commitment in the program is to register participants and/or to have them sign a formal agreement. This agreement is usually a simple statement the spells out the choices the young person has made and explains how important his or her commitment to the program, the meetings, etc., is. This technique helps the young person take the program seriously.

Step 9

Evaluating the Curriculum

Evaluation is an essential and often forgotten step. At the completion of a faith theme learning plan, a season, semester or quarter, and the entire year, evaluations should be conducted. The young people, the catechists/religion teachers, coordinators and administrators, should all be involved in evaluation. [Chapter 8 in this Manual provides you with several sample evaluation forms. Be sure to adapt them for your particular situation.]

Further Resources on Leader Development

Bannon, William and Suzanne Donovan. *Volunteers and Ministry.* New York, NY: Paulist. 1983.

Johnson, Douglas. *The Care and Feeding of Volunteers.* Nashville, TN: Abingdon. 1980.

The Ministry of Volunteers. Office of Church Life and Leadership. St. Louis, MO: United Church of Christ. 1979.

Rauner, Judy. *Helping People Volunteer.* San Diego, CA: Marlborough Publications. 1980.

Wilson, Marlene. *How to Mobilize Church Volunteers.* Minneapolis, MN: Augsburg. 1983.

Worksheet #1:

Foundational Principles of Adolescent Catechesis

Worksheet #1 assists you in assessing how well the five foundational principles guide your curriculum. Review the five principles (see Chapter 1 in this Manual) and complete the questions below. Your reflections will be shared, forming the basis for a profile of how these principles are being applied.

● How does your present adolescent catechesis program demonstrate a commitment to lifelong catechesis? [*Principle #1*]

_____

_____

● How does your present adolescent catechesis program promote Catholic Christian faith in three dimensions: trusting, believing, doing? Which is most prominent in your curriculum teaching? Which is most lacking? [*Principle #2*]

_____

_____

● How does your present adolescent catechesis program support, encourage, and involve parents/families? [*Principle #3*]

_____

_____

● How does your present adolescent catechesis program demonstrate respect for and build upon the cultural heritages of your youth? How does your curriculum respond to the unique learning needs of youth of different cultures? [*Principle #4*]

_____

_____

● How is your model integrated into the total parish or school ministry with youth? [*Principle #5*]

_____

_____

a. Identify the principles that are functioning well in your catechetical ministry.

_____

b. Identify the principles that need to be functioning more effectively in your catechetical ministry.

_____

Operational Principles of Adolescent Catechesis

Worksheet #2 assists you in assessing how the five operational principles are being implemented in your curriculum. Please review the five operational principles (see Chapter 1 in this Manual) and complete the questions below. Your reflections will be shared, forming the basis for a profile of how these principles are being applied.

- How does your present adolescent catechesis program respond, in practice, to the developmental, social, cultural needs of adolescents? [*Principle #6*]

  _____
  _____
  _____
  _____
  _____

- How does your present adolescent catechesis program respect the variability in maturation and learning needs of adolescents? If your model uses age-grading, how does it account for the variability in maturation and learning needs of youth? [*Principle #7*]

  _____
  _____
  _____
  _____
  _____

- How does your present adolescent catechesis program respect the expanding freedom and autonomy of adolescents? Does your model allow youth freedom to choose the faith themes that best respond to their learning needs? [*Principle #8*]

  _____
  _____
  _____
  _____
  _____

- How does your present adolescent catechesis program utilize a variety of learning formats, environments, schedules, and educational techniques? List them below. [*Principle #9*]

  _____

  _____

  _____

  _____

  _____

- How does your present adolescent catechesis program organize courses or topics? Do you utilize a faith themes approach? Or is it another approach, like the survey approach? [*Principle #10*]

  _____

  _____

  _____

  _____

  _____

a. What obstacles, from your own experience, hinder the implementation of the operational principles?

  _____

  _____

  _____

  _____

b. Check the three primary obstacles hindering implementation.

  _____

  _____

  _____

  _____

Worksheet #3:

Taking Stock of the Catechetical Program

Directions: On this worksheet, list the ways (courses, retreats) that you are currently teaching each faith theme (in younger and older adolescence). Then evaluate how effective you think you are in addressing the scope and content of the theme. On the scale, 1 is poor and 5 is very good. (Review the faith themes by consulting Chapter 2 of this Manual or *The Challenge.*)

I. Younger Adolescent Themes						
a. Church Programs/Learning Model:	Evaluation:	1	2	3	4	5
b. Jesus and the Gospel Message Programs/Learning Model:	Evaluation:	1	2	3	4	5
c. Moral Decision-Making Programs/Learning Model:	Evaluation:	1	2	3	4	5
d. Personal Growth Programs/Learning Model:	Evaluation:	1	2	3	4	5
e. Relationships Programs/Learning Model:	Evaluation:	1	2	3	4	5
f. Service Programs/Learning Model:	Evaluation:	1	2	3	4	5
g. Human Sexuality Programs/Learning Model:	Evaluation:	1	2	3	4	5

II. Older Adolescent Themes

a. Faith and Identity Programs/Learning Model:	Evaluation:	1	2	3	4	5
b. The Gospels Programs/Learning Model:	Evaluation:	1	2	3	4	5
c. The Hebrew Scriptures Programs/Learning Model:	Evaluation:	1	2	3	4	5
d. Jesus Programs/Learning Model:	Evaluation:	1	2	3	4	5
e. Justice and Peace Programs/Learning Model:	Evaluation:	1	2	3	4	5
f. Love and Lifestyles Programs/Learning Model:	Evaluation:	1	2	3	4	5
g. Morality Programs/Learning Model:	Evaluation:	1	2	3	4	5
h. Paul and His Letters Programs/Learning Model:	Evaluation:	1	2	3	4	5
i. Prayer and Worship Programs/Learning Model:	Evaluation:	1	2	3	4	5

Youth Hearings

Process for Youth Hearings

Materials needed: Name tags; newsprint, markers, masking tape for each small group, Needs Assessment Tool #1 or #3, opening and closing prayer service.

Time Frame: 1½–2 hours.

Set-up: Chairs organized into groups of 8.

1. **Orientation** (10 minutes)

   a. Welcome All Participants to the Hearing

   b. Rationale and Overview of the Hearing Explain the role of the hearings in the overall curriculum planning process; how the input from the young people will be used in planning a catechetical program; and why listening to their needs is so important. Explain the role of the adult leaders: they will serve the young people as small group facilitators and recorders.

2. **Group Building and Prayer** (20 minutes)

   a. Form the young people randomly into groups no larger than six–eight.

   b. Conduct a very brief community building activity so that the young people can get to know each other's name and a little about each person in the group.

   c. Lead the participants in a brief prayer service.

3. **Youth Concerns Activity** (30 minutes)

   Focusing Question: "What do you think are the most important concerns of young people today?"

   a. *Individual Reflection:* Allow the young people three–five minutes to reflect on the question.

   b. *Group Work:* Ask each person in the group to share his or her concerns and ask the recorder to write all the concerns on newsprint (10 minutes).

   c. *Discussion:* Allow 10 minutes of discussion on the concerns that were shared by the participants. At the conclusion of the discussion, ask each group to put an asterisk or check in front of the concerns it felt were the most important. (Another way to identify the most important Concerns is to give each young person 3 or 4 votes and to record those votes on newsprint, and then tally the results to determine the top priorities of your group). You might want to circle the top priority concerns so that they will be easy to see.

   d. *Post and Observe:* Ask each group to post its newsprint sheet on the wall and then given the participants five minutes to mill around reading the other group priorities.

4. **Youth Needs Assessment** (30 minutes)

   a. *Questionnaire:* Distribute Tool #1 or 2 to each young person. Give them 10 minutes to answer the questionnaire. (You may want to count out eight surveys for each group in advance.)

   b. *Reflection:* Ask each young person to select four or five of the most important needs or topics from the questionnaire.

   c. *Discussion:* Ask the participants to share their top four or five needs with their group. The recorder should be listing the number of responses each need receives. In advance, the recorder should prepare a newsprint sheet listing the question numbers and a key word for each question. Then all that has to be done is record the number of responses for each need (10 minutes).

   d. *Reporting:* Each group then posts their results on the wall for all to see. Give the participants five minutes to review the other reports.

Be sure to collect all the questionnaires so that a profile can be developed.

7. **Closing Prayer and Thanks** (5 minutes)

Needs Assessment Tool #1

Adolescent Catechesis Interest Finder: Youth

Instructions: This Interest Finder gives you a chance to make yourself heard about a variety of programs and activities that might be available through your church. Read each statement and decide whether or not it is something you would like. Circle the number which best reflects your interest.

Age _____   Grade _____

	none	some	much	very much
1. Find out what is special about me.	1	2	3	4
2. Better understanding of my parents, and learn how to communicate with them.	1	2	3	4
3. Learn the skills form making and keeping friendships.	1	2	3	4
4. Learning what it means to be a Catholic.	1	2	3	4
5. Learning how to deal with drugs and alcohol.	1	2	3	4
6. Understand my sexuality better.	1	2	3	4
7. Learn the Christian views of sex, dating, and marriage.	1	2	3	4
8. Learn to speak naturally and intelligently about my faith.	1	2	3	4
9. Find meaning and purpose in my life.	1	2	3	4
10. Learn to understand the Old Testament better and what it means to us today.	1	2	3	4
11. Learn to understand the New Testament better and what it means to us today.	1	2	3	4
12. Experience a closer relationship with God.	1	2	3	4
13. Be of service to other people in my community and the world who need help.	1	2	3	4
14. Learn about what is right and wrong and how to make moral decisions as a Christian.	1	2	3	4
15. Develop a deeper understanding of the life and message of Jesus.	1	2	3	4
16. Learn about the Christian's response to social problems like hunger, war.	1	2	3	4

	none	some	much	very much
17. Learn how to forgive others and be a peacemaker in my relationships and in the world.	1	2	3	4
18. Learn how to pray in a personal way.	1	2	3	4
19. Plan and participate in a variety of worship and prayer services.	1	2	3	4
20. Learn how to deal with the pressures people place on me (friends, teachers, parents).	1	2	3	4
21. Learn how to deal with the problems I face as a young person.	1	2	3	4
21. Learning to understand the sacraments better and their meaning for us today.	1	2	3	4
22. Learn about adult lifestyles (marriage, religious vocation) and how to make life choices.	1	2	3	4
23. Learn about the Church of today and what it means to belong to the Church today.	1	2	3	4

Program Scheduling
(For Parish Programming)

a. Days of the Week:

Please indicate the best days of the week for your participation in programs that the parish would sponsor. Check *all* the days that are good For you!

———— Sunday Afternoon

———— Sunday Evening

———— Monday Evening

———— Tuesday Evening

———— Wednesday Evening

———— Thursday Evening

———— Friday Evening

———— Saturday

———— Saturday Evening

b. Frequency of Meetings

Please indicate how frequently you would participate in programs that the parish would sponsor. Select *all* the options that are good for you!

———— Every week

———— Every other week

———— Once a month

THANK YOU!

Needs Assessment Tool #2

Adolescent Catechesis Topical Ranking

This Topical Ranking gives you a chance to identify the topics for this year's catechetical program that you are most interested in. Read over the entire list and then decide which topic is of most interest to you by rating it #1. Then proceed through the list to your last choice.

Age _____   Grade _____

_____ Discovering what is unique about me

_____ Developing skills for making and keeping relationships

_____ Developing a more personal relationship with Jesus

_____ Learning how to make moral decisions

_____ Understanding my sexuality

_____ Discovering what it means to belong to the Church

_____ Being involved in service to other people

_____ Developing a personal prayer life

_____ Exploring the life and message of Jesus

_____ Developing a personal moral value system

_____ Exploring adult lifestyles (marriage, single life)

_____ Exploring the Old Testament

_____ Exploring the Gospels

_____ Exploring the Letters of Paul

_____ Discovering what it means for me to be a Catholic

_____ Exploring the Christian response to the social problems and injustice in our world

Program Scheduling
(For Parish Programming)

A. Days of the Week:

Please indicate the best days of the week for your participation in programs that the parish would sponsor. Check *all* the days that are good for you!

_____ Sunday Afternoon

_____ Sunday Evening

_____ Monday Evening

_____ Tuesday Evening

_____ Wednesday Evening

_____ Thursday Evening

_____ Friday Evening

_____ Saturday

_____ Saturday Evening

B. Frequency of Meetings

Please indicate how frequently you would participate in programs that the parish would sponsor. Select all the options that are good for you!

_____ Every week

_____ Every other week

_____ Once a month

THANK YOU!

Needs Assessment Tool #3

Interest Finder Survey: Parents of Youth

This Interest Finder gives you a chance to make yourself heard about a variety of programs and activities that might be available for you and for your teenager(s) through the parish in the coming months.

Age of Teenager(s) and Grades: _____ _____ _____

A. Please indicate your interest in the following programs that help parents learn: (circle the number)

	none	some	much	very much
1. More about drugs & alcohol and how to help my teenager deal with them.	1	2	3	4
2. How to communicate better with my teenager.	1	2	3	4
3. How to help my child develop healthy concepts of right and wrong.	1	2	3	4
4. How to help my child grow in faith.	1	2	3	4
5. More about education in human sexuality.	1	2	3	4
6. How to discipline effectively my teenager.	1	2	3	4
7. More about the growth during teen years.	1	2	3	4

B. Please indicate how important you think it is for the parish to offer the following programs for teenagers:

[V = Very Important; I = Important; U = Unimportant (Circle one)]

V I U   1. To help young people learn the skills for how to make and keep friendships.

V I U   2. To guide the development of faith and Catholic values in young people.

V I U   3. To assist young people in developing a healthy self-concept.

V I U   4. To teach young people what is right and wrong and how to make moral decisions as Catholics.

V I U   5. To teach young people to pray.

V I U   6. To assist young people in forming a responsible Catholic approach in sexual matters.

V I U   7. To involve young people in reaching out to serve people in need.

V I U   8. To help young people develop a deeper appreciation of Jesus' life and message.

V I U   9. To help young people develop a better understanding of the Bible and what it means to us today.

Worksheet #4:

Designing a Faith Theme Learning Plan

1. Faith Theme:

_____

_____

2. Focus:

_____

_____

_____

3. Topics:

_____

_____

_____

4. Learning Objectives:
At the conclusion of this faith theme the learner should be open to:

Trusting: _____

_____

_____

_____

Believing _____

_____

_____

_____

Doing: _____

_____

_____

_____

5. Learning Model:

_____

_____

_____

6. Setting:

_____

_____

_____

7. Dates: _____ **8.** Time: _____

9. Number of Sessions: _____ **10.** Number of Participants _____

11. Possible Materials/Resources:

_____

_____

_____

12. Leaders Required:

_____

_____

_____

13. Learning Experience Designers:

_____

_____

_____

Sample Learning Plans

The following sample learning plans demonstrate how to utilize the curriculum planning process. Both examples use the gospels faith theme, but develop the theme in different ways.

Example #1—Parish

1. **Faith Theme:** Exploring the Gospels **(Older Adolescence)**

2. **Focus:** This learning experience will engage the young person in learning how to interpret the gospels as a Catholic Christian. The older adolescent will explore the historical and literary development of the gospels; and the structure, major themes and explore the unique presentation of Jesus and the Good News in the gospels.

3. **Topics:** Three stages of gospel development, how to read a gospel, background of each gospel author and his community, structural outline of each gospel, key themes of each gospel, portrait of Jesus in each gospel, literary forms used in each gospel.

4. **Learning Objectives:** At the conclusion of this faith theme the learner should:

Trusting:

a. have experienced the support and acceptance of the group

b. have discovered specific ways to live the gospels in developing a closer relationship with Jesus, especially in his/her prayer life.

Believing:

a. be able to describe the historical and literary development of the gospels within the Catholic Christian tradition

b. be able to describe the structure, major themes and unique presentation of Jesus in each gospel.

Doing:

a. apply the skills of interpreting a Gospel

b. have discoverd concrete ways to follow Jesus based on the study of thegospels.

5. **Learning Model:** Six week mini-course; two hours per session

6. **Setting:** Either church meeting room or home of catechist.

7. **Dates:** Wednesdays, October 9 through November 13

8. **Time:** 7:30-9:30 P.M.

9. **Number of Sessions:** Six

10. **Number of Participants:** 15 maximum

11. **Possible Materials/Resources:**
    - catechetical resources for teaching the gospels
    - youth booklet
    - refreshments for each session
    - possible use of film, filmstrip or video during the program
    - materials for closing prayer experiences

12. **Leaders Required:** One or two catechists

13. **Learning Experience Designers:** Catechists with DRE or CYM.

Example #2 — School

1. **Faith Theme:** Exploring the Gospels **(Older Adolescence)**

2. **Focus:** This learning experience will engage the young person in learning how to interpret the gospels as a Catholic Christian. The older adolescent will explore the historical and literary development of the gospels; and the structure, major themes and explore the unique presentation of Jesus and the Good News in the gospels.

3. **Topics:** Three stages of gospel development, how to read a gospel, background of each gospel author and his community, structural outline of each gospel, key themes of each gospel, portrait of Jesus in each gospel, literary forms used in each gospel.

4. **Learning Objectives:** At the conclusion of this faith theme the learner should:

Trusting:

a. have experienced the support and acceptance of the group

b. have discovered specific ways to live the gospels in developing a closer relationship with Jesus, especially in his/her prayer life.

Believing:

a. be able to describe the historical and literary development of the gospels within the Catholic Christian tradition

b. be able to describe the structure, major themes and unique presentation of Jesus in the gospels.

Doing:

a. apply the skills of interpreting a gospel

b. have discoverd concrete ways to follow Jesus based on the study of the gospels.

5. **Learning Model:** Semester course as part of the core curriculum; action-learning through the service project; prayer/worship

6. **Setting:** Classroom, chapel, and community (for service project)

7. **Dates:** First Semester

8. **Time:** 3rd Period

9. **Number of Sessions:** 50 sessions; 1 hour per session

10. **Number of Participants:** 25 per class

11. **Possible Materials/Resource:**
    - catechetical resources for teaching the gospels
    - student text
    - film, video, filmstrip *materials for prayer experiences
    - community organizations for service projects.

12. **Leaders Required:** Religion teacher, and contact people for service projects, campus minister for service programming and prayer services.

13. **Learning Experience Designers:** Religion teacher and campus minister.

Leadership Development

Leader Tasks Worksheet

Program	Leadership Tasks	Needed Leadership Positions
a. _____	1. _____	Position: _____
	2. _____	(Task #'s _____)
	3. _____	(Task #'s _____)
	4. _____	(Task #'s _____)
	5. _____	(Task #'s _____)
b. _____	1. _____	Position: _____
	2. _____	(Task #'s _____)
	3. _____	(Task #'s _____)
	4. _____	(Task #'s _____)
	5. _____	(Task #'s _____)
c. _____	1. _____	Position: _____
	2. _____	(Task #'s _____)
	3. _____	(Task #'s _____)
	4. _____	(Task #'s _____)
	5. _____	(Task #'s _____)
d. _____	1. _____	Position: _____
	2. _____	(Task #'s _____)
	3. _____	(Task #'s _____)
	4. _____	(Task #'s _____)
	5. _____	(Task #'s _____)

[List as many tasks as needed. List as many positions as needed.]

Leadership Development

Job Description Worksheet

1. **Program:** _____

   Job Title: _____

2. **Leader Tasks to Be Performed:** [List them.]

   a. _____ e. _____

   b. _____ f. _____

   c. _____ g. _____

   d. _____ h. _____

3. **Abilities Needed:** (skills, attitudes, understanding)

   a. _____ e. _____

   b. _____ f. _____

   c. _____ g. _____

   d. _____ h. _____

4. **Involvements:** (Other commitments, additional responsibilities, additional meetings) [List them.]

   _____

5. **Length of Commitment:**

   Service From: _____ To: _____

   Meetings: _____

   Training: _____

6. **Supervision/Support:** (Who? When?)

   _____

7. **Training Required:** (When? How can it be obtained?)

   _____

8. **Benefits of the Position to the Leader:**

   _____

9. **Leader Responsible To:**

   _____

Leadership Development

Sample Job Description For a Catechist

1. Program:
Older adolescent catechetical program
Job Title: Catechist for a mini-course

2. Leader tasks to be performed:

a. Designing and conducting the mini-course learning program.

b. Obtaining the materials needed to conduct the program from the Coordinator of Youth Ministry.

c. Evaluating the learning program.

d. Contact youth who miss sessions.

e. Report to the CYM on the progress of the program.

3. Abilities Needed: (See: *The Challenge,* Part V, p. 17)

a. Ability to design a learning experience using shared Christian praxis.

b. Ability to use media in a learning program.

c. Willingness and ability to speak with conviction about his or her own experience and convictions as a Catholic Christian.

d. Understanding of adolescent growth and development, (especially faith growth).

e. Understanding of the signs, symbols, images, and culture of youth.

f. Ability to lead a group discussion and conduct faith sharing activities.

g. Ability to design and conduct prayer experiences.

h. Understanding of the content of his or her particular faith theme.

4. Involvements: Participation in support group meetings.

5. Length of commitment: Total = 12 meetings (weeks)
Service From: September 1
To: November 15

Meetings: Two planning meetings in September; six teaching sessions (Oct.1-Nov. 15); one catechist support meeting; one evaluation meeting.

Training: For new catechists—two workshops in September.

6. Supervision/Support: Catechist support group meeting; weekly contact with coordinator of youth ministry.

7. Training required: Two planning meeting and two pre-service workshops (new catechists *only*) in September.

8. Benefits of the position to the leader:
Opportunity to share his or her faith with youth; to guide youth in their growth as a Catholic Christians; to be challenged to grow as an adult Catholic; to receive the support of other adult leaders.

9. Leader responsible to: Coordinator of youth ministry.

Leadership Development

Recruiting Leaders Worksheet

Realizing that my time and talents must be made available if the Church is to fulfill responsibly its call to be engaged in continuing the mission and ministry of Jesus Christ, I hereby indicate my desire to dedicate a portion of my time and services to youth ministry in the area(s) checked in the list below. I understanding that assignment to any specific tasks will be made only after appropriate consultation and with prayerful deliberation. (Please check *ALL* the areas you would be willing to serve in.)

Name _____ Phone _____

Address _____

Age _____ Occupation _____

Business Address _____ Bus. Phone _____

List Special Training _____

_____

_____

Hobbies _____

Interests _____

Active in What Church Ministries _____

_____

Active in What Community Organizations _____

_____

I would be glad to serve in adolescent catechesis in the area(s) of:
[List your leadership positions in adolescent catechesis and youth ministry.]

Time you have available for adolescent catechesis:

Hours per week _____ Regularly each week: _____ Yes _____ No

Preferred days/evenings _____

Signature _____ Date _____

Curriculum models provide an overall framework for organizing the faith themes into a coherent schema. The models offered in this chapter are meant to serve as guides in developing your own model. Each model described seeks to apply the operational principles of adolescent catechesis presented in *The Challenge.* They offer alternatives to age-graded approaches. They use developmental and social growth as means for planning catechesis. They provide a framework for offering a variety of learning topics to respond to the learning needs of adolescents. They provide opportunities for adolescents to select the topics and formats for learning. They offer a framework in which catechetical planners can develop a curriculum with variety in format, environment, schedule, and educational technique. Each framework uses the faith themes approach as outlined in *The Challenge.* Be sure to *adapt* these models to your particular setting. They are meant as guides to help you.

Model 1 Electives

The elective model is based on offering young people choices from a variety of faith themes programmed in different formats, environments, and scheduling. The key in this model is *variety.* In parish settings, there is so much competition for young people's time and involvements that a youth ministry must be very creative in offering formats, environments and schedules that respond to the life situation of young people. The elective model can provide the curriculum model that allows this to happen. This model is similar to a university which offers a variety of courses on different topics, at different times, and often at different locations to meet the needs of its students.

By providing well-written and interesting course descriptions and by providing guidance to young people as they select learning topics, this model gives young people the variety to find a topic that meets their needs and is offered when they can attend. The key in this model is offering enough variety to both respond to the adolescents' needs and to attract them to participate.

This catechetical curriculum model can easily be integrated into a comprehensive youth ministry or campus ministry, by organizing the entire youth ministry around a variety of elective programs in Prayer and Worship, Guidance and Healing, Justice and Service, Evangelization, Community Life, and Enablement. Young people then choose from this variety of programs based on interests and schedules (family, school, work). In this model it is extremely important that each program (and each faith theme) be adequately described and creatively named so that young people can select the ones for them.

Another important element of the electives approach to a comprehensive youth ministry is seasonal programming. The easiest way to program the electives model is on a seasonal basis of three—four month blocks (fall-winter-spring-summer). Each season will need to begin with a opening night which includes community building, a time to sign-up or register for programs, and social activities. A booklet should be prepared describing all the courses and providing a registration sheet for the catechetical courses and/or all youth ministry programs. Several weeks later the actual programming begins. This gives time for the leaders to organize the young people's participation based on the registrations and to assign them to the first, second or third choices for catechetical courses and/or other programs.

The following example reflects a parish setting. This example could easily be revised for a Catholic high school to reflect the courses of the religion curriculum and the programs of the campus ministry. This outline would form the basis of developing a season booklet of program offerings.

Catechesis

a. Six-Week Mini-Courses
(Drawn from younger and older adolescent themes, offered on different nights of the week, at the parish center or in homes.)

1. Following Jesus
2. Growing as a Moral Person
3. Exploring the Gospels
4. Becoming a Mature Sexual Person
5. Love and Lifestyles
6. Living and Doing Justice

b. Special Prayer Program:
Learning How To Pray
(a one-to-one, spiritual direction approach to learning how to pray; meets every other week).

c. Weekend Program for Juniors and Seniors: Faith and Identity.

Community Life

a. Bi-weekly youth gatherings for all young people with community building, social activities, and specifically designed programs, often using outside speakers and media.

b. Regularly scheduled social and recreational events.

Guidance and Healing

a. Three-session, parent-teen communication workshop.

b. Special youth gatherings (Community Life) focusing on key adolescent concern (substance abuse, suicide).

c. One-to-one counselling and referral service (through the parish and through agencies in the community).

Justice and Service

a. Six-week mini-course: Living and Doing Justice (Catechesis).

b. Ten service projects for youth to choose from in the parish and community, lasting 6–10 weeks.

c. Hunger awareness week: workshops and action projects.

Worship and Prayer

a. Special prayer program: Learning How To Pray (Catechesis).

b. Thanksgiving worship service—worship planning team needed.

c. Advent worship services—before each youth gathering in Advent—worship planning team needed.

Enablement

Peer ministry training program—two weekend training program followed by a year-long commitment to ministry; anyone who wants to participate must complete an application form.

Model 2 Focus Areas

This second curriculum model owes much to the process of faith growth outlined in the Rite of Christian Initiation of Adults (*RCIA*). The journey of the person through the RCIA process begins with *evangelization*—a time of awakening faith through hospitality, storytelling, proclaiming the Good News, and guiding people in developing a personal relationship with Jesus Christ. The second period of the RCIA is the *catechumenate*—a time of deepening faith through a multi-dimensional catechesis involving instruction, community and liturgical participation, apostolic action, and sponsorship. The third period of the RCIA is the time of *purification* and *enlightenment* or the consecration of faith in which the person now participates in an immediate and intensive preparation for the reception of the sacraments of Initiation [Baptism, Confirmation, Eucharist]. The fourth period is the time of *post-baptismal catechesis.* The person has celebrated the sacraments of Initiation and is engaged in a deepening of his or her sacramental experience and preparation for ministry within the community.

In adapting this process to ministry with youth (in parishes or schools) leaders have developed four programs of catechesis, corresponding to the four periods of the RCIA. Each phase presents a more in-depth presentation of the Catholic Christian faith. They have organized the faith themes of younger and older adolescence into several focused programs:

1. Focused on introducing young people to the Christian faith (evangelization);

2. Focused on greater depth and challenging them to growth as Christians;

3. Focused on a coherent exploration of the heart of the Christian message;

4. Focused on Christian lifestyle and spirituality.

In order to respect the variability of adolescent development and the variety of learning needs, young people are guided in selecting the focus that addresses their learning needs and their faith growth at this particular time in their journey. This may mean interviewing each young person and/or providing complete (and interesting) descriptions of each focus or course so that the young people can select their learning program. Each phase can be developed into one entire learning program (or course) or into several learning programs (courses). *All four focus programs need to be offered simultaneously since young people are at different points in their faith journey.* These focus areas should not be programmed into grade levels or viewed as sequential for all young people. Some young people will move from focus 1 through focus 4, but many, because of their readiness, will be ready for a more in-depth catechesis.

The following is offered as a guide for developing your curriculum based on this model of progressive growth in faith.

Focus 1: Evangelization

This is a highly relational program that introduces young people to the gospel in an attractive manner. Evangelization builds a spirit of community in the group and establishes relationships of trust between the young people and their adult leaders. Evangelization involves storytelling, helping young people discover their own story of faith and to experience the stories of the gospel and Christian tradition. As young people discover their own story of faith, they can begin the process of relating that story to the stories of others, of the parish, of the Scriptures, of the Tradition. Evangelization guides young people in developing a personal relationship with Jesus Christ, in the midst of the Christian community. The younger adolescent faith themes of Personal Growth, Relationships, Jesus, and Church help to cover the core content for this evangelization phase.

Focus 2: Initial Catechesis

This second focus builds upon evangelization and calls the young people to greater depth, challenging them to reflect on what it means to grow as Christian persons. Initial catechesis provides the young people with the opportunities to explore the implications of their growth in Christian maturity. The younger adolescent faith themes of Sexuality, Moral Decision-Making, and Service help to cover the core content of initial catechesis.

Focus 3: In-depth Catechesis

The third focus offers young people an integrated exploration of the very heart of the Christian message—Jesus and the Gospel he proclaimed, along with the way in which that message is lived out and celebrated in the life of the Church today. Many of the topics of Focus 1 and 2 are explored again, but this time with a new depth that responds to the adolescent's growing faith. The older adolescent faith themes of Jesus, Morality, Hebrew Scriptures, The Gospels, Paul and His Letters, and Justice and Peace help to cover the core content of this phase.

Focus 4: Christian Lifestyle

Focus four helps young people reflect on the implications of their Christian faith for the lifestyle and vocational decisions that confront them in the later adolescent years and young adulthood. The older adolescent faith themes of Prayer and Worship (Spirituality), Love and Lifestyles, and Faith and Identity help young people prepare for future growth as Catholic Christians.

Model 3 Core Curriculum With Electives

A third approach to organizing the faith themes using the framework of a distinct catechesis for younger and older adolescents is a core curriculum with electives. There are two variations of this model:

1. a core curriculum for 9th and 10th grades, with electives for 11th and 12th grades, and

2. a limited core and electives for both 9th and 10th grades, and 11th and 12th grades. Like the other models, it is extremely important that each faith theme be adequately described and creatively named so that young people can select the electives which best meet their learning needs.

The first option in organizing such an approach is to develop a 9th and 10th grades' core curriculum with electives for 11th and 12th grades. This model is built on the assumption that certain learning needs are addressed in the early stages of the curriculum before individual interests can be satisfied in the later stages of the program. The core curriculum for 9th and 10th grades utilizes many of the faith themes for younger adolescents (Church, Jesus and The Gospel Message, Moral Decision-Making). All 9th and 10th graders would be required to take this series of courses. They could be offered in a sequence that all young people would take or offered so that young people would select the order they wish to take the courses. The latter option would mean that teachers could be assigned one or two courses of the core curriculum to teach, rather than teaching all the courses of the core (former option). Juniors and seniors would then select courses from the variety of quarter or semester-long elective courses drawn from the older adolescent themes (Gospels, Hebrew Scriptures, Justice and Peace, Love and Lifestyles).

A second option is a core curriculum and electives for 9th–10th and 11th–12th grades. This model is built on the assumption that it is essential to address certain younger adolescent themes and certain older adolescent themes before individual interests can be satisfied through electives. For example, the core for 9th and 10th grades might consist of two semester-long required courses (e.g. Jesus and The Gospel Message, and Moral Decision-Making) with elective courses of a quarter or semester duration on a variety of themes (Church, Personal Growth, Relationships, Service, and Human Sexuality). The core curriculum for 11th and 12th grades might consist of two courses (the Gospels, and Justice and Peace) with elective courses (Faith and Identity, Hebrew Scriptures, Jesus, Love and Lifestyles, Morality, Paul and His Letters, Prayer and Worship).

Chapter 5

Learning Models for Adolescent Catechesis

There are a variety of learning models available for use within adolescent catechesis. The following descriptions are intended to help you select the best model for your learning objectives, setting and time. An effective catechetical program will utilize a variety of learning models, thus offering young people the opportunity to learn in a variety of ways. Several of the models are possible only in a parish setting. Most can be applied to parish and school settings. While parishes may have less restrictions regarding selection of models, a school setting can find the variety of models described here to be very useful if they can adopt flexible scheduling. Flexible scheduling is probably the greatest aid to utilizing a variety of learning models in a school setting.

Action-Learning Model

Action-learning can take the form of study followed by action, involvement in a service project followed by reflection and study, or awareness and analysis followed by action and reflection. In each of these formats, action-learning focuses catechesis on the learning which is a by-product of action or a means to increase the effectiveness of action. Involvement in a soup kitchen, nursing home for the elderly, food center, hunger walk, advocacy work on human rights or hunger can all lead to reflection and further study of the issues of justice, peace, aging, poverty, hunger. The action can be either a catalyst for learning or an expression of the learning. Often, young people are involved in service but do not have the opportunity to reflect on the experience and opportunities for further study. Many youth ministries organize mission projects, work camps, or service projects. Each of these action projects has a catechetical component either leading to action or out of action. In many schools students are involved in a study/action

course one afternoon per week (with periodic reflection meetings) as an integral part of their four-year catechetical curriculum.

Bi-Weekly Model

In the bi-weekly model, sessions are scheduled every other week usually for a longer time span (for example, three hours) so as to allow sufficient time for community building. A typical six–eight session course would take three–four months to complete. The bi-weekly model allows other youth ministry programming to take place on the alternate weeks. Some parishes have organized their younger adolescent course offerings on the first and third weeks of the month, and their older adolescent course offerings on the second and fourth weeks of the month.

A bi-weekly model is effective with all adolescents. Younger adolescents respond well to the bi-weekly model when it is integrated with other youth ministry programming on the alternate weeks, thereby offering them variety. Older adolescents may find it difficult to schedule themselves over three–four months, but this model does give them the alternate weeks off.

Full Day Model

The use of the full day model has increased significantly in adolescent catechesis. The full day model brings young people together for an extended period of study, reflection, interaction, prayer and action/service. This model may be used in a five to eight hour session. It often includes a shared meal, a liturgical celebration, and informal socializing. In the full day model there are two or three learning sessions lasting 1½—2 hours each. Several full day programs can be grouped together on one theme (like a mini-course) or scheduled five or six times throughout the year each with a distinct theme.

Full day programs call for careful planning. It is recommended that a team of leaders (both adults and young people) meet well in advance to plan each of these days. Some items to be considered are: previewing resource materials; selection of a date with as few conflicts as possible; choosing of a location which provides a pleasant environment; planning for snacks and meals, assignment of catechists/facilitators for each part of the day; preparing for liturgy or prayer service.

A full day model is effective with all adolescents. The length of the day should be accommodated to the abilities of the younger adolescent, especially regarding the intensity of the schedule and nature of the theme. Older adolescents can sustain the intensity of the full day model and it responds well to their life situation in which they will make short-term commitments. You can accomplish in one day what could have easily taken three weekly meetings to accomplish.

Individualized Learning Model

The individualized learning model can be programmed on *one-to-one individualized study* plan or can be programmed in a *learning centers* format. The one-to-one option can be used to explore a particular theme that attracts the participation of a small number of youth or that best lends itself to one-to-one programming. Many parishes and schools have established courses aimed to help young people develop a personal prayer life using a spiritual director model. The spiritual director and young person meet weekly or bi-weekly over the course of two or three months to pray, share insights on praying and reflect on the young person's experience of praying as he or she is guided in developing a personal prayer life. Not only is this course best suited to one-on-one but it does not depend on large numbers enrolling.

Learning centers provide another approach to individualized learning that can be used with large groups of young people. A learning center is a setting containing a collection of activities and materials to teach and/or enrich a skill or concept. The setting is a total learning environment with resources and space organized for learning, usually with a separate station for each activity being offered. Pre-programmed activities and materials placed in a center are designed to teach a specific skill or concept, and thus they are based on specific learning outcomes. A learning center usually includes several stations that cover a topic or aspect of a topic, a concept, or a group of skills. Materials and instructions at each station are carefully planned so that adolescents can work through them in accord with their own learning styles and pace. Therefore, adolescents have the opportunity to take responsibility for their own learning, pursue their own inquiry through a variety of learning activities.

Resources:

Blake, Howard. *Creating a Learning-Centered Classroom.* New York: Hart Publishing Co, 1977.

Kilgore, Lois. *Eight Special Studies For Senior Highs.* (108 Learning Centers) Scottsdale, AZ: National Teacher Education Project (6947 East MacDonald Drive, 85253), 1976.

The Learning Center Approach Revisted. United Church Board for Homeland Ministries. (DECEE, Box 179, St. Louis, MO 63166)

Using Learning Centers in Church Education. St. Louis, MO: Joint Educational Development, United Church of Christ (P.O. Box 7286, 63177).

Intergenerational Model/Parent Education

The intergenerational model brings together youth and their parents or entire families for catechesis. The **family-centered catechesis** program is best geared for children and younger adolescents. It may not be effective with older adolescents. Developing a family-centered catechesis will involve addressing the faith themes of younger adolescence within a family context. This can be done by parents, by catechists, by special speakers, etc. Family-centered catechesis can also be integrated with liturgical celebrations, creating a well-rounded program.

Youth-Parent Programming will respond well to all adolescent needs. This catechesis can take a variety of forms to meet learning needs that youth and adults have in common: parent-youth suppers with a specially designed program or speaker, mini-courses (specially designed program or speaker), service programming where parents and youth study and act on a common social concern, family activities and programs which build communication, trust, and closeness, parent-teen programs that discuss moral values and promote discussion, worship and scripture resources for parents to use in the home, parent-teen retreat experiences, home-based advent and lenten programs (as individual families or clusters). Above all, youth-parent programming should be well focused and short-term.

One way to integrate parents into the adolescent catechesis curriculum is to design certain courses with parent sessions built right in. A course on human sexuality (a great course to involve parents) might begin with a parents-only session, followed by three youth sessions, another parents-only session, three more youth sessions, and finally a parent-teen closing session.

Parent Education is an integral element for catechetical planners to build into an entire adolescent catechesis program. Parent education may include specific learning experiences designed for parents around their learning needs and concerns as parents: information on adolescent growth, skills for communication and for parenting, contemporary moral teachings, moral decision-making, how to communicate moral values, contemporary Church teachings. Second, it can be built into a course for adolescents by offering several parent-only sessions. For example, a course on morality might include three sessions specially designed for parents on the topics covered in the youth course (a session before, during, and at the conclusion of the youth course).

A third option is to develop a parallel curriculum for parents using the themes of the adolescent curriculum, but developed around the learning needs of adults. Parents can take an adult course (morality, scripture), while their son or daughter is taking an adolescent course on the same topic. For many parishes/schools this is the beginning of an adult education curriculum. You can adapt the curriculum design process in this Manual to help you develop a parent education program. Parent education programs need time to gain recognition. Small numbers in the beginning is not an indication that parent education is not needed. Over the course of several years, parent education programs can become a well-respected and well-attended part of your programming.

Resources:

Griggs, Donald and Patricia. *Generations Learning Together.* Nashville: Abingdon, 1978.

Dalglish, William. *The Family Centered Model.* Nashville: Board of Discipleship, United Methodist Church, 1974.

Family-Centered Catechesis. Washington, DC: USCC/Department of Education, 1979.

Koehler, George. *Learning Together.* Nashville: Discipleship Resources, 1977.

Sawin, Margaret. *Hope for Families.* New York: Sadlier, 1982.

Mini-Course Model

The mini-course model can become the bread-and-butter of parish catechetical programming for adolescents. Whether you are using a weekly, bi-weekly, full day, overnight, weekend, or full-week model, you can use the mini-course model. This model organizes the faith themes into four-six-eight session course offerings. Mini-courses can be offered throughout the year, allowing time between mini-courses for the variety of other youth ministry programming. Many parishes conduct mini-courses on a six-eight week basis in the fall, winter and spring—allowing plenty of time for other programming. Other parishes conduct the first three weeks of a six week mini-course, then take a meeting for community building, special event and/or worship, and then resume the mini-course for the second three weeks.

Schools can use the mini-course model by using shorter, quarter-long courses rather than semester-long courses. The inter-term model (see below) offers a way to program mini-courses into a regular semester-basis curriculum. The mini-course approach allows for electives and more focused learning experiences, thereby enhancing variety in the curriculum.

Monthly Model

The monthly model can be used in two ways: monthly meetings or monthly full day programming (described above). In the monthly meeting approach, sessions are scheduled for a longer time span (three-four hours) so as to allow sufficient time for two learning sessions, community building, prayer, etc. A typical six-eight session course would take three to four months to complete. The monthly model allows other youth ministry programming to take place during the month. Many parishes gather young people monthly (often because of distance) for four hours, offering them a variety of faith themes taught as mini-courses to select from, as well as providing them with time for socializing and community prayer.

A monthly model is effective with all adolescents. Younger adolescents respond well to the monthly model when it is integrated with other youth ministry programming on the alternate weeks, thereby offering them variety. Older adolescents find it easier to schedule themselves once a month. One of the drawbacks of the exclusive use of the monthly meeting model can be the infrequent contact among the young people. This can be overcome by offering a variety of youth ministry programming during the month.

Overnight Model/Weekend Model

One of the most effective models for fostering adolescent faith growth over the last twenty years has been the weekend retreat. The weekend model utilizes many of the dynamics of the retreat weekend—extended time for the building of relationships, the forming of community, sharing of religious experiences, prayer and liturgical experiences—all for catechetical purposes. The weekend model fosters faith growth through the integration of educational, communal(social/recreational/interaction), and religious experiences. Using the weekend model means that there are six, 2–2$\frac{1}{2}$ hour learning sessions available to catechetical planners. (The overnight model makes available three-four, 2–2$\frac{1}{2}$ hour learning sessions.) In addition, time for community building, recreation, liturgy and prayer must also be scheduled.

Like the full day model, the overnight/weekend model calls for careful planning. It is recommended that a team of leaders (both adults and young people) meet well in advance to plan the weekend.

A weekend model is most effective with older adolescents. They can sustain the intensity of the weekend model and it responds well to their life situation in which they will make short term commitments. You can accomplish in a weekend what would easily take you six weekly meetings or two to three full day programs to accomplish. In general, the length and intensity of the weekend places many demands on the younger adolescent that he or she may not be able to sustain. Sophomores are usually able to handle the weekend model. You will need to use your own judgment regarding adolescents who are younger.

The overnight model responds well with all adolescents. The overnight model is quite applicable to the younger adolescent. You will need to use your own judgment regarding the proper age for this type of experience.

Camping trips provide another model for catechesis. Organized with the same care as a Weekend Model, camping trips provide an outdoor setting for catechesis.

Seasonal Model

The seasonal model organizes the catechetical program using either fall-winter-spring-summer seasons or liturgical seasons—Advent and Lent. The seasons of the year help to organize the catechetical program in three or four month units. Within these units, the various catechetical offerings are organized. The liturgical seasons offers two regular times during the year for catechesis. These Advent and Lenten offerings can easily parallel parish-wide programs. They also offer the possibility of integrating liturgy, study, parish involvement, and service into a concentrated time span and thereby tapping the richness of the Advent or Lenten season.

Small Group/Learning Team Model

The small group model has become popularized in such renewal programs as RENEW, in the Rite of Christian Initiation of Adults (*RCIA*), and in the Base Community movement in Latin America. Parishes have adapted this model by offering young people the opportunity to group themselves with a catechist around a particular theme or emphasis. For example, parishes have offered young people a multi-track catechesis—organizing the faith themes of younger and older adolescence into several focus groups: one track geared toward introducing young people to the Christian faith (evangelization); one track geared to greater depth and challenging them to growth as Christians; one track geared to a coherent exploration of the heart of the Christian message; and one geared to Christian lifestyle and spirituality. This approach then encourages young people, with the help of the catechists, to group themselves according to their growth in faith. These small groups remain together for an entire year or more—building community, learning together, serving together and prayer together. There is an emphasis in the small group model on an integrated approach in which catechesis is connected with community, service, and worship.

Spiritual Reflection Groups Model

Many schools have developed a spiritual reflection component in their regular classes. Students have class three times a week. Two sessions use the regular classroom format. The third session is conducted in groups of twelve. The teacher meets with these groups of twelve on three different days. The small size group allows for discussion, personal sharing and guided prayer.

Study Tour/Trip Models

The study tour model offers catechetical planners the ability to use learning opportunities outside the parish or school community. One course on the Judaeo-Christian tradition was designed by visiting each of the churches/synagogue in town, listening to a presentation by the minister/rabbi, and touring the church/synagogue. Another course on Church visited a variety of Catholic churches in urban, suburban and rural areas to explore how they were organized and the variety of their ministries. This course also explore the ministries of the diocesan Church (for example, social ministry). Such tours provide opportunities for first hand experience and can be combined with classroom presentation, discussion, and reflection.

Week-Long Model/Inter-Term Model

There are parish and school versions of the week-long model. For **parishes,** the *first option* for week-long programming is a weeknight program for three to five nights, $1\frac{1}{2}$–2 hours per night. This option takes the weekly meeting model and condenses the time frame into one-week. Parishes which use this option, offer several mini-courses in this time frame and repeat these week-long mini-courses throughout the year. The big advantage of this option is concentration and continuity. It takes careful planning, especially in selecting weeks which do not conflict with community or school events, or with exams or special tests at school. You may want to even clear the dates with the school

and parish administration so that nothing will be scheduled on these special week-long catechetical programs.

The *second option* is a full day (and possibly overnight) week-long program during school vacations or summer. Many parishes have adapted the vacation bible school concept to their younger adolescent catechetical program—offering several thematic courses in three–four weeks during the summer. In addition to morning and afternoon learning sessions, there is time scheduled for recreation and socializing. This three-four week summer program supplants the usual catechetical program during the year—allowing time during the year for a variety of youth ministry programming. A second variation on this full day option is similar to summer camp—young people spend an entire week at a retreat or camp site studying, recreating and interacting. One or two faith themes can be offered during a week-long program.

The first variation above responds well to the younger adolescent who is not working at a summer job, while the second variation responds to all adolescents.

For **schools,** an inter-term, one or two week special program offered before the spring semester, and after the fall semester affords the opportunity for variety in scheduling and learning model. In-school catechesis with prayer and worship can be combined with action-reflection projects and study tours/field trips in this model.

Weekly Model

The weekly model may be the most commonly used approach to adolescent catechesis in parishes and schools, but it is not the only approach. In parishes, courses are scheduled for a series of meetings (six–eight weeks per course) on weeknights or Sunday evenings. Sessions can be designed to last $1\frac{1}{2}$ to 2 hours. Anything less than $1\frac{1}{2}$ hours is not desirable with adolescents. Keeping in mind our curriculum principles, a weekly meeting model should be short-term (six–eight sessions). Courses can be offered throughout the year.

The timing of programs following this model makes a difference. Some parishes find it better to have these sessions following the same schedule as the school semesters in their area. Other parishes prefer to organize the program into distinct blocks of four, six, or eight weeks for which the adolescents enroll each time around. The description of the seasonal and mini-course model explains this "block approach" to programming.

A weekly model is more effective with younger adolescents who tend to participate more regularly and who respond better to shorter time frames than do older adolescents. Older adolescents find it increasingly difficult to make commitments for six to eight consecutive weeks. This can be overcome by scheduling three to four week offerings. The selection of other learning models for later adolescents will help address this concern.

Worship/Celebration Model

Like the fellowship model, the worship/celebration model offers a context for catechesis. The *first context* involves young people in liturgy planning and, as a consequence, the adolescents will be involved in studying and reflecting on the Scriptures; studying the meaning of liturgy: the rites, the symbols; and planning liturgy—the ways the message of the Scriptures affects song selection and prayers. Whether it involves planning for a Sunday or seasonal (Thanksgiving) or special event (senior graduation) liturgy planning offers a marvelous opportunity for catechesis.

A *second context* for catechesis is within a celebration (church season or special event). For example, the celebration of Pentecost can be the context for catechesis on Church. At the homily, the young people can be organized into

small groups and explore a particular faith theme, like Church (perhaps the mission and characteristics of the early Church as described in the Book of Acts). The results of that learning can be shared at the Presentation of Gifts—through creative art, gesture, song, and audiovisual. If the adolescents are also involved in planning the liturgy, this celebration will become a tremendous learning experience.

A *third context* is a weekly catechetical program based on the Sunday Scripture readings. This program can be conducted after the Sunday Eucharist or on Sunday evening or in school on Monday. Using the Sunday readings, a theme is developed which connects the life experience of the adolescent with the Scriptures. Through activities, discussion, and reflection the meaning of the Scriptures are applied to the life of the adolescent.

Youth Fellowship Model

A youth fellowship can be defined as an informal setting in which youth and their adult advisors participate on a regular basis (usually weekly) in a program that includes key elements such as learning activities, recreation/community building, worship, and service projects. The fellowship model integrates learning activities into an overall program that is less formal than many other settings. The fellowship model tries to provide balance among the four key elements, providing that balance at each meeting or over the course of a month or three-month period. This model provides a context for catechesis. The catechesis is often scheduled as a one-theme per meeting or one theme developed over several meetings in the course of three months. Some parishes even provide options for study—offering one theme geared to older adolescents and one theme for younger adolescents.

Choosing the Best Learning Models:
A Checklist (Sample)

1. Assess the personnel and budgetary resources available.

2. Evaluate the faith needs of the young people in the parish.

3. Determine the potential conflicts in scheduling, availability of learning facilities in the area.

4. Enlist the cooperation of parish/community administrators and supervisors who will help to facilitate the learning models chosen to be used.

5. Include the parents of the adolescents in structuring and supporting the learning models to be utilized.

6. Ensure the facilities made available for adolescent catechetical learning reflect the invitation to grow in the Catholic faith as a maturing person.

6

Learning Process in Adolescent Catechesis

How do we share with young people the Good News of Jesus Christ and the wisdom of the Catholic Tradition in ways appropriate to their development, culture, language and symbols and, at that the same time, in ways that will lead to understanding, reflection, and transformation? This may well be *the* central question in adolescent catechesis today. *The Challenge of Adolescent Catechesis* offers a process for adolescent catechesis that seeks to connect the life-world of youth with the Catholic Christian tradition.

"The fundamental process of adolescent catechesis involves discovering the relationship among the Catholic Christian tradition; God's present activity in the life of the adolescent, family, community, and world; and the contemporary life experience of the adolescent" (p. 8). This process is a dialogue between the life-world of the adolescent, with its joys, struggles, questions, concerns, and hopes and the wisdom of the Catholic Christian tradition. Effective catechesis is in tune with the life situations of youth—their language, lifestyles, family realities, culture, and global realities. But, effective catechesis does not stop here. It creatively and imaginatively presents the Christian message so that young people can understand it and interpret their life situation in light of it. This means that catechesis will challenge young people with the demands of Christian discipleship.

The process described above can be translated into all of our catechetical efforts. We can design learning experiences, retreat experiences, programs which embody the central dynamic of engaging the life of the adolescent with the Christian tradition and fostering the kind of interaction that helps young people reflect on the wisdom of the tradition. Thomas Groome in *Christian Religious Education* has described a learning process

which embodies a contemporary approach to catechesis. This learning process begins with the life experience of the young person, engaging him or her in critical reflection on that experience, and then relating that experience to the Scriptures and Tradition. The process concludes by engaging the young person in reflecting on the meaning of the Scriptures/ Tradition for his or her life and what the implications of these meanings are for his or her belief and lifestyle. The entire learning process can span one session, several sessions, or an entire course.

Here is a overview of the five movements of shared Christian praxis drawn from the work of Thomas Groome. [For further reading on shared Christian praxis consult, *Christian Religious Education* by Thomas Groome (Harper & Row, l981), especially chapters 9 and 10.]

Focusing Activity

The purpose of the *focusing activity* is to bring the attention of the group to bear on the theme of the lesson or session so that the young people can begin to identify it in their own life, their family, culture, society, church. The focusing activity is meant to grab the attention of the young people through an experiential learning activity. We are trying to help the young people look at their own activity (beliefs, values, attitudes, understanding, feelings, and doing) around the theme for the session. Some learning experiences need very short focusing activities because the topic is easy to draw out from their life experience and concerns (topics like sexuality, personal growth, relationships, moral dilemmas). Other times we will need to be very creative to draw them into the topic because it may, on the surface, seem removed from their current life experience and concerns (Scripture, prayer and worship, justice and peace).

The focusing activity can be programmed in a number of ways. For example: group activity, story, poem, rock music and videos, a project, Scripture reading, role playing, field trip, movie/video, simulation game, creative art, case study, demonstration, reflection questionnaire.

Movement One: Experiencing Life

Having focused young people on the topic/concept of the learning experience as it is already present in their own life experience, *Movement One* invites them to express themselves concerning this life experience. Movement One enables the young people to express their own life activity (knowing, action, feeling) or that of their community, ethnic culture, youth culture, dominant culture or society on the topic or concept of the learning experience. Young people are encouraged to express what they already know about the topic/concept, or how they feel about it, or how they understand it, or how they now live it, or what they believe about it.

Inviting the young people to express their life experience on the topic of the learning experience can be accomplished in a variety of ways: presentations, reflection questionnaires, drama/role playing, making and describing something, symbolizing or miming. Helping young people express their present action needs to done in a non-threatening way. Always make it clear that the young people should feel free to share or simply to participate by listening. Be sure to leave time for silence.

Movement Two: Reflecting Together

The purpose of *Movement Two* is to allow the young people an opportunity to reflect together on what they have expressed in Movement One about their own experience/activity. This will sometimes be intuitive as well as analytical. Movement Two engages reason, memory, and imagination. This is often done by sharing an actual story of their experience or an action they have taken. Young people are invited to reflect critically on the meaning of their own experience —share the consequences of their present experience/action and implications for the future.

An important element of Movement Two is engaging the young people in interpreting their life experience in the broader picture of their families, ethnic culture, youth culture, dominant culture and society. Each of these contexts influences the shape of their life. We need to engage young people in a critical reflection on the impact that society and culture have on their values and lifestyles. Young people are influenced by the media (through TV, commercials, music and videos) and the values of the dominant culture in the United States. Through critically reflection, young people are able to name the impact on their life. On many subjects, like sexuality and morality, we must deal with the messages young people receive from media and the dominant culture or else the Christian message will not be heard. We cannot name these influences for young people; we can guide them to reflect critically on these influences, name them for themselves, open them to the Christian vision of life, and help them make decisions about values, attitudes and lifestyles.

Movement Three: Discovering the Faith Story

Movement Three presents the Story and Vision of the Catholic Christian community in response to the topic or concept of the learning experience. The *Story* is a metaphor for the whole faith identity of the Christian community. Here the young people encounter the Story of faith that comes to us from Scripture, Tradition, the teachings of the Church, and the faith-life of Christian people throughout the ages and in our present time. The *Vision* is a metaphor for what the Story promises to and demands of our lives. It is God's Vision of God's Reign (the Kingdom of God). We engage young people in exploring how we are called to live faithfully God's Vision, individually and as a community—at the personal, interpersonal, and social/political levels of human existence.

From a Christian faith perspective, it is within the *Story* and *Vision* that we interpret, make sense out of and respond to our own stories and vision. In Christian faith, our own stories must be interpreted within the Christian Story—in dialogue with it. Our own visions must be critiqued and lived within the Christian Vision—in dialogue with that Vision.

Sharing the Story is accomplished through a variety of means—presentations, guided study (of the Scriptures), media (film, filmstrip, music), reading, discussion, research, field trip, group project, demonstration, or panel presentation. We seek to involve both the teacher and the learner in sharing the Story and exploring the Vision. Young people need to be actively involved in Movement Three. We should not encourage passive reception of the Story and Vision.

It is important to keep in mind the following points as you prepare Movement Three:

1. The *Story* shared reflects the most informed understanding the community (magisterium, scholars, faithful) knows at this time;

2. The *Vision* proposed and the Story shared promotes the values of God's Reign in people's lives—peace, justice, love, freedom, life, and wholeness;

3. The *Story* and *Vision* engages the participants—touching the focus, stories, visions of their lives as expressed in the Focusing Activity and Movements One and Two.

Movement Four: Owning the Faith

Movement Four provides the young people with an opportunity to compare their own life experience and faith with the Story and Vision of the Catholic Christian community. Through this dialogue young people can test out their experience and their experience can be informed by the Christian Story and Vision. The Story will confront, challenge, affirm, and/or expand the faith of young people. The purpose of Movement Four is to enable the participants to take the Story and Vision back to their own life situations, to appropriate its meaning for their lives, to make it their own. It attempts to promote a moment of "aha" when the participants come to know the Story as their own, in the context of their lives.

There will be as many responses to this dialogue as there are young people. It is vitally important at this step to allow the young people the freedom to come to their own answers and conclusions. With this freedom young people can be guided to see the "why" of the Christian Story and Vision.

Movement Four can be accomplished in a variety of ways: reflection questionnaire comparing movement one and two responses with the movement three story; creative expression of one's learning by writing; creating a role play or a dramatization or a case study; creating an audio-visual presentation (video, slide show); creating a symbol or poster; group activity/discussion; imagination activities where young people envision how they can live out the learnings from the session.

Movement Five: Responding in Faith

The purpose of *Movement Five* is to help bring young people to a lived faith response. By inviting young people to decision, the fifth movement aims to help them translate their learning into a lived faith response. Once again, applying the learning from the learning experience must be a free response. Some young people will be changed by the learning experience and motivated to concrete action, while others will need time to ponder its meanings and implications, and still others will not be affected by the learning experience. We must provide an environment which invites a faith response, a decision for living more faithfully as a Christian, but which also respects the right of young people to choose their own response, even if it is not the response we had hoped for.

Responding in faith will affect the three levels of human existence: the personal, the interpersonal/ communal, and the social. To help young people respond in faith, we need to probe the implications of their learning for all levels of life. We can engage them in developing three of these concrete plans for the coming week (personally, interpersonally, socially); in individual or group action projects which involve them in living their faith (action in the faith community, school, family, community/ society); in prayer experiences which celebrate or draw young people into reflection on their response; in journaling activities where they can reflect on how they are living their faith.

Shared Christian Praxis Worksheet

This worksheet can assist you in designing learning experiences using the shared Christian praxis approach.

Focusing Activity

a. What is the particular focus of your learning experience?
b. What is your focusing question/activity for this learning experience?
c. How will you engage the participants in identifying their present action?

Movement One:
Experiencing Life

How will you engage the participants in expressing their own life activity (knowing, action, feeling) or that of their community, culture or society that underlines the theme, topic or concept of the learning experience?

Movement Two:
Reflecting Together

a. How will you engage in the participants in telling a story(s) that explains their present action?
b. How will you engage them in critically reflecting on their present action in light of the broader picture?
c. How will you engage them in identifying the consequences of their action and the implications for future living?

Movement Three:
Discovering the Faith Story

a. What Story(s) will you present? What Vision will you offer? Does it reflect the most informed understanding of the community?
b. What resources will you use?
c. How will you creatively and imaginatively present the Story and Vision?

Movement Four:
Owning the Faith

How will engage the participants in a dialogue between their story and the Story and Vision of the Christian community?

Movement Five:
Responding in Faith

In light of the entire learning experience, how will engage the participants in deciding on what action to take (personally, interpersonally, socially/politically).

For Further Study

Griggs, Donald. *Teaching Teachers To Teach.* Nashville, TN: Abingdon Press. l974.

_____ . *Planning for Teaching Church School.* Nashville, TN: Abingdon. 1985.

Groome, Thomas. *Christian Religious Education.* San Francisco; Harper and Row. 1981.

Little, Sara. *To Set One's Heart.* Atlanta: John Knox Press. l983.

Chapter 7

A Survey of Learning Methods for Adolescent Catechists

Developed by Reynolds R. Ekstrom

Establishing Learning Environments

The much respected educational leader, Malcolm Knowles, cautions us that good teachers, do not just happen—they set out on the path of becoming competent as well as compassionate, well-grounded in the principles and techniques of learning and well-versed in understanding human conditions that deeply affect the learning situation. First and foremost, catechists who work with adolescents must establish environments in which teaching and learning can truly take place. Trust among young learners and their catechists, and among the learners themselves must develop. They must be able to listen, discuss and create together. There should be enough trust and comfort in the situation that new insights and new directions, freely discovered, can be applied to lives of all.

Catechists of youth often hear youth complain, "It's boring," or "I don't get anything out it." While catechists are heard to say, "I can't get them involved," "I can't hold their attention," and "I don't know what else to try." There are no magical catechetical methods that remedy the discipline and disinterest problems sometimes encountered. Yet, the setting or environment for the catechetical activity is critical. The catechist must develop a learning space in which all learners are encouraged to be fully present and to be fully involved.

Do such learning environments really exist? Yes, in parish youth centers, in catechists' homes, in church basements, in classrooms, almost anywhere the following conditions exist:

1. Individual learners can bring their full selves (real thoughts, feelings, questions, relationships, and life experiences) rather than only their "correct," always-proper selves.

2. Learners and catechists feel safe and free in speaking up, in expressing doubts and questions, in sharing joys, victories, struggles, and feelings, and respecting that things will be shared in confidence.

3. The gathering place or class site is physically comfortable and safe for all; outside noise, lighting, heat, cold, or decoration should not hinder the learning process.

4. In an atmosphere of friendship, welcome, and trust, the catechist sets an expectant tone that says, "Something meaningful is going to happen here today if we all work together."

Experiential Learning

The teaching activities employed in such learning situations deserve careful attention. Inexperienced catechists often wonder at first, "What should I tell the class about God (or the church, sacraments, prayer, morality)?" It is the wrong first question. One should reflect on "What will the learners and I do together on the topic _____ ?" This leads the catechist to think about teaching activities which will urge learners to reconsider their assumptions and acquire new learning.

One way to visualize the variety of teaching activities is Edgar Dale's "Cone of Learning." Dale explains the cone as follows:

> Looking at the cone, you see that each division represents a stage between the two extremes—between direct experience and pure abstraction. If you travel upward from the base, you move in the order of

decreasing directness . . . Similarly, if you travel downward from the pinnacle of the cone, you move in the order of increasing directness: "verbal symbols" are more abstract than "visual symbols"; and "visual symbols" are more abstract than such "one-sided aids" as recordings, radio, and still pictures.[1]

As you can see the movement from top to bottom is a movement from the more abstract to the more concrete, from less involvement by the learners to more direct involvement.[2]

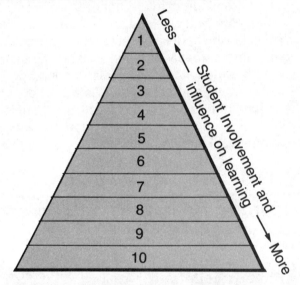

Here are examples for each category of Dale's Cone of Learning.

1. **Verbal Symbols**—storytelling, reading, sermon, lecture, debate, dialog, interview, group interview, panel, discussion;

2. **Visual Symbols**—books, pictures, maps, charts, photographs, art, diagrams, cartoons;

3. **Audio Symbols**—records, cassettes, radio;

4. **Audiovisual Symbols**—films, filmstrips, videotapes, music videos, slide shows, television;

5. **Exhibits**—displays, bulletin boards, posters;

6. **Field Trips**—in the community, to other churches;

7. **Demonstrations**—by resource people;

8. **Dramatized Experiences**—plays, scripts;

9. **Contrived Experiences**—role playing, simulation games, case studies;

10. **Direct, Purposeful, Personal Experiences**—service projects, mission work camps, prayer, worship, creative expression (creating videos, slide shows, scripts, role plays, case studies), creative writing.

Evidence suggests that most people do not learn well by simply listening in a passive way. Verbal activities should be directly linked with other learning experiences. Using verbal, visual and audio-visual symbols together leads to more effective learning than when these activities are used alone. Dramatized and contrived experiences help learners act on feelings, issues, problems or beliefs they hold by acting something out, as if it were for real. These non-threatening experiences help young people to understand and identify with certain viewpoints, or to grasp deeper learning on important concepts. Direct, purposeful, personal experiences involve learners in real life situations. Learners acquire the most knowledge and insight from direct, meaningful experiences, especially when this is combine with the other methods. As you plan your learning experience and develop learning objectives, you can match objectives with appropriate methods.

Knowledge: Generalizations about experience, internalization of information.

Methods: Lecture, television, debate, dialog, interview, symposium, panel, group interview, colloquy, motion picture, video, film, audio cassette, book-based discussion, reading.

Understanding: Application of information and generalizations.

Methods: Audience participation, demonstration, film, video, dramatization, problem-solving discussion, case discussion, critical incident process, case method, simulation games, instruments.

Skills: Incorporation of new ways of performing through practice.

Methods: Role playing, simulation games, structured experiences, participative cases, skill practice exercises, drill, coaching.

Attitudes: Adoption of new feelings through experiencing greater success with them than with old ones.

Methods: Experience-sharing discussion, group centered discussion, critical incident process, case method, simulation games, participative cases, non-verbal exercises.

Values: The adoption and priority arrangement of beliefs.

Methods: Television, debate, dialog, symposium, colloquy, film, video, dramatization, guided discussion, experience-sharing discussion, role playing, critical incident process, simulation games, instruments.

Interests: Satisfying exposure to new activities.

Methods: Television, film, video, demonstration, dramatization, experience-sharing discussion, exhibits, trips, non-verbal exercises.[3]

To guide your selection of methods for your learning experience, the catechist should keep these points in mind:

1. The method(s) used should help the catechist communicate clearly the key religious content of the learning experience.

2. The method(s) should be appropriate to the developmental readiness, interests, and abilities of the learners. The learners be comfortable with the method(s) selected.

3. In any learning experience, a variety of creative methods should be employed.

4. The method(s) should fit with the time, space, and resources or equipment you have.

5. The catechist needs to be comfortable with the method(s) selected and posses the skills required.

6. The learners should be involved experientially in active and purposeful ways, allowing for maximum creative expression.

7. No activity should be over-used so as to bore or frustrate the learners.

8. Learners should be encouraged to be creative, original, and enthusiastic in performing each learning activity.

9. Each method used should draw learners toward new questions, new conclusions, and creative responses in faith.

Adolescent catechesis helps foster change and growth toward maturing in faith. As a learning process, it sponsors young people toward a genuinely-lived Christian faith. It takes place in an environment which encourages mutual trust, human freedom, comfort, honesty, and community. Catechists utilize techniques and activities which, deliberately and intentionally, get learners deeply involved in exploring their own life experiences and in discovering how God is active and present for us all. A key aspect of the faithful catechist's task, then, is to become more skilled, more comfortable with experiential learning methods.

Learning Methods for Adolescent Catechesis

Bible Encounter

The group leader selects and proclaims a passage from Scripture. Learners are then encouraged to ask questions about the passage or to respond to what they have heard. Each learner then is challenged to respond, in writing, to "What would have to happen in my life if I were to take these Bible verses seriously?" Learners share responses in small groups and report back to the overall group.

The catechist:

a. selects Bible passage to be used or selects it along with several group members before the session;

b. urges each group member to write a paraphrase of the Scripture verses;

c. then challenges learners to write a response to "What would happen if I took these verses seriously?";

d. reorganizes the learners into small groups;

e. asks each person to share a paraphrase and response to the reflection question;

f. reassembles the whole group; calls for reports from small groups and for any individual contributions to be made;

g. summarizes input and insights that have surfaced; then challenges participants to act on what they have discovered.

The learners:

a. must understand what is expected of them;

b. reflect on the Bible passage and re-write it;

c. respond to the reflection question in writing;

d. share their thoughts and writing with members of the small group;

e. further clarify their insights in the ensuing discussion;

f. listen carefully to others' contributions;

g. decide which Christian action(s) will help them put their new insights and discoveries into practice.

Brainstorm (Idea Inventory)

The group leader suggests a problem or question to those gathered. The group rapidly suggests solutions, all of which are recorded on newsprint or a chalkboard. No idea or solution is to be subject to criticism or negative comment. Once a list of solutions/answers is complete, the items on the list are reflected on.

The catechist:

a. identifies the problem or question the group will face;

b. appoints someone to record responses;

c. asks participants to provide responses in quick succession, contributing any/all constructive solutions that come to mind;

d. urges group members not to criticize or otherwise evaluate solutions at first;

e. sets a limited period of time for the brainstorm;

f. calls for solutions/answers to the problem at hand;

g. leads the group in reflection on and evaluation of the items surfaced.

The learners:

a. reflect seriously on the central problem or question;

b. contribute verbally any constructive ideas/ solutions that come to mind;

c. withhold comments and evaluations on brainstormed items until all suggestions have been made;

d. participate in the group's reflection on and evaluation of solutions offered;

e. help determine how insights might be used.

Buzz Groups

The leader divides a full group into smaller groups of three-six persons for a very limited period of time. (The activity can also be done in pairs, or dyads.) Small groups discuss (or "buzz") on assigned question or problem. A reporter—selected in each buzz group—reports his/her small group's findings to everyone.

The catechist:

a. provides the question or issue for discussion;

b. divides the full group into smaller, "buzz" groupings (three-six persons each);

c. sets a time limit (often 5 minutes or less per question) for groups to accomplish the task;

d. asks each buzz group to pick a reporter;

e. defines the question/issue and goal clearly;

f. circulates among buzz groups to see that they function effectively;

g. tells groups when they have one minute remaining in their discussions;

h. calls time and re-gathers full group;

i. requests a report from each buzz group;

j. calls for comments from participants;

k. summarizes verbally some key findings and asks others to also cite key insights;

l. proposes appropriate study/action when feasible.

The learners:

a. can be asked to help in identifying a problem or issue;

b. select a reporter for each buzz group;

c. reflect on and seriously discuss the topic at hand;

d. pay attention to the contributions of others;

e. contribute appropriately when in the full group;

f. help determine how buzz group insights should be further studied or put into action.

Case Study

The group leader reveals some information regarding a true-to-life situation. Group members analyze the situation—its problems, its potential—and develop solutions.

The catechist:

a. prepare a case study, or case story, about one or more persons, recording data on the following points: the people involved, the historical background; the relationships between those involved, the religious background of those involved, sociological factors, economic factors, the educational background of those involved, their ethnic origins, the tensions or issues involved;

b. helps participants to scrutinize the case;

c. summarizes the group members' insights and invites others to add their summaries;

d. reflects aloud on how the information and insights might be applied to learners' lives.

The learners:

a. might help in selecting and preparing the case study;

b. listen to the data and reflect on the case study carefully (either individually or in small groups);

c. determine the real issue(s) or problem(s) present in the case study;

d. suggest some solutions or answers to the issue/problem;

e. identify pros and cons of each potential solution;

f. identify the most appropriate solution(s); provide reasons for selecting each solution;

g. contribute summary statements on the learning acquired through this activity.

Circle Sharing

The overall leader invites all participants to reflect on a particular question or concern. The group (twelve or less) is seated in a tight circle, or if large (thirteen or more) is divided into smaller circular groups. Each participant, moving one by one around the circle, is able to voice a response. No one speaks a second time until all have had one opportunity.

The catechist:

a. helps participants arrange their chairs (or themselves) in one or more circles;

b. invites responses to a particular question or concern;

c. urges each group member to respond;

d. models how to respond, by going first;

e. asks person to the right to also respond, then, urges each other person, one by one, to likewise respond;

f. challenges participants to contribute added comments or to then take part in an open discussion;

g. summarizes chief insights and learnings;

h. suggests ways to further reflect on or to act on new learnings.

The learners:

a. provide individual responses to the question or concern at hand;

b. pay close attention to the statements of others;

c. help determine how new information and insights is to be studied or used;

d. add freely to group's reflection beyond the basic sharing-circle responses.

Collages and Posters

A collage is a composite of printed matter, original lettering, and pictures and symbols affixed (usually glued) to a surface, for example, a posterboard. A collage is a creative learners' response to a specific topic, subject, or issue. It crystallizes the learners' ideas on the topic.

The catechist:

a. helps learners clearly identify the topic;

b. helps them understand the purpose and process of constructing a collage;

c. reassembles the full group into smaller, creative teams or urges learners to work individually and provides magazines, newspapers, markers, glue, other materials;

d. invites learners to display and discuss their creative work; asks questions about each piece and invites deeper discussion on each by the full group;

e. summarizes key contributions by individuals/ teams.

The learners:

a. engage in individual or group work on collages;

b. select appropriate magazine or newspaper pictures, symbols, and/or printed words for their artwork; add appropriate hand-lettering to materials to be used;

c. collaborate with others, as team members, when appropriate;

d. describe the meaning and intent of their work to other learners;

e. answer questions about and receive comments on their work;

f. probe and discuss the artworks of others in the group;

Creative Writing

(see also Drawing and Writing in Groups)

The group leader invites learners to engage in some original, creative writing on some particular topic (What is God like? or, What will the future bring?). This writing can take various forms: poems, other rhymes, short stories, newspaper articles, journal entries, or essays. Usually this writing focuses on or illustrates some religious concept being studied by the group. It provides learners with an opportunity to express their feelings and ideas on subject matters in a special way. Creative writing can be an active, effective response or supplement to another teaching activity: a lecture, a discussion, viewing a film or video, or participation in a role-play.

Discussion Groups

A group of learners gather to discuss and reflect cooperatively upon a topic of interest. In the process, they express ideas and opinions, share insights, seek new data, and learn from one another. Each discussion group needs a leader. Sometimes that person is skilled or trained in discussion techniques, sometimes not.

The overall leader of the discussion:

a. helps to identify the topic(s) for consideration;

b. sets the environment, arranging furniture and materials so that all participants can face one another;

c. encourages learners to prepare for the discussion;

d. develops questions and/or statements that will open (and guide) the discussion;

e. welcomes all, then poses the problem(s) or issue(s) to be addressed;

f. helps set the goal(s) of the discussion group;

g. suggests the set of questions or guiding statements, and a timeline, to the group;

h. urges all members to contribute actively;

i. attempts to keep the discussion on track;

j. makes an effort to get all members to contribute to the dialogue;

k. clarifies points, provides needed summaries, re-calls the group to questions at hand when appropriate;

l. avoids making speeches, but contributes to the discussion process in a constructive way;

m. summarizes key insights, thanks all for their contributions, suggests further study or courses of action, and closes the experience.

The discussion group participants:

a. can be invited to help identify the main topic or particular questions to be considered;

b. prepare appropriately for the dialogue;

c. help to define the goal(s), ground rules, and time line for the experience;

d. reflect seriously on the questions at hand;

e. listen carefully to the ideas of others;

f. contribute their own ideas and attempt to build upon the insights of others;

g. respect others involved in the entire process;

h. assist others by clarifying or adding to statements already made;

i. speak up only when there are meaningful, relevant ideas to contribute;

j. when possible, summarize key insights or new learnings arising from the dialogue;

k. determine personal needs for further study or reflection and decide how new information might be acted on.

Drawing and Writing in Groups

The leader separates the full group into small units of three-five persons each. Each small group then decides upon some central ideas or learnings about an assigned subject. Working as a team, the small group expresses its ideas/ learnings in a drawing or through a poem, paragraph, news release, telegram, or other creative writing. The small groups' drawings or writings are later shared and discussed with the whole group.

The catechist:

a. proposes a topic or subject for the creative expressive and forms full group into small units;

b. reads or displays some examples of appropriate, creative responses to the challenge;

c. gives small groups ample time to work;

d. encourages maximum sharing and creative interchange in the smaller groups;

e. provides necessary materials for artwork;

f. calls small groups together and asks each to share its written or drawn response;

g. urges all participants to respond to and discuss each group contribution;

h. summarizes key insights and themes that have surfaced during the experience;

i. asks group members to reflect on and share what this activity has meant to them.

The learners:

a. listen to and observe types of appropriate responses (written or drawn) presented as examples;

b. reflect seriously on the topic at hand;

c. contribute freely to discussion of the topic;

d. join and participate fully in a small group;

e. help decide how to express the ideas/ learnings of the group in a creative way;

f. do some writing or drawing for the small group if called upon;

g. help the small group share its work with the full group of learners;

h. ask questions about, reflect on, or otherwise comment on the contributions of other participants;

i. reflect on the meaning of this learning experience.

Field Trips

The learning group journeys to various places to come into contact firsthand with sources of information. It exposes learners to immediate experiences of people, places and things.

The catechist:

a. prepares for the trip by making preliminary arrangements as necessary, describes the purpose of the trip to the group, shares data about the site, and suggests appropriate ground rules for behavior and activity at the site;

b. while at the site to be visited, introduces group members to their guide(s), maintains overall responsibility for the group at throughout the trip;

c. after the field trip, challenges learners to discuss and interpret their learnings and asks them to report on the whole experience and helps learners summarize and evaluate the field trip process then, suggests possible further study or Christian action.

The group members:

a. should be adequately prepared and clear about the purpose of the trip;

b. prepare for the field trip according to the suggestions made by the group leader;

c. pay attention to the guide(s) at the site visited, question and seek clarifications when additional information is desired;

d. participate in discussion and interpretation of the entire experience;

e. summarize and evaluate the meaning of the field trip;

f. help determine areas for further study or Christian action based upon the trip;

Interviews

In an attempt to stretch beyond our minimal time with learners, we sometimes seek to involve them in activities during periods when the learning group is not together. The interview method for learning deliberately sends learners out to encounter other persons. The goal is that they will gain information and perspectives from these persons which will be of benefit to the learners as a whole. Thus, the outside interview solicits information about a topic, beyond the usual boundaries of the group. But it also causes the learner to become directly involved in gathering and acquiring data, in trying to organize and interpret it, and in presenting his or her findings to the whole group.

The catechist should remind learners about the following before they do their interviews:

a. don't be a bother or be rude to the person sought for an interview;

b. be honest about your purpose in contacting the potential interviewee and agree to a good time for him or her or the interviewee's own "ground rules";

c. become like an earnest reporter when conducting the interview;

d. do some basic reading ("homework") on the interview-topic before the meeting;

e. keep the interview brief; concentrate on asking a handful of good questions and on recording good answers received;

f. be willing to "play it by ear" for the interviewee may suggest ideas or questions beyond your original ideas for the interview, then explore new avenues of interest which crop up during the interview.

As group leader, make contact with the interviewers during the time they should be completing the interviews. Call them or talk to them about how they are doing. Encourage, support, and advise as necessary. Help those who might be experiencing problems in doing their project.

Lecture Forum

The group leader, an outside resource person, a learner, or a video-presentation delivers a lecture to a learning group. This is immediately followed by a free wide-open discussion (a forum) involving all group members.

The speaker:

a. presents material verbally in an engaging style;

b. seeks questions and comments from learners and encourages dialogue among listeners;

c. summarizes key points and makes suggestions about how to use the information presented;

The group members:

a. listen carefully to input from speaker;

b. take appropriate notes on key points;

c. ask questions of or make comments to the speaker when so requested;

d. participate in an open discussion on key lecture points, among all participants, when speaker has concluded;

e. determine how new information could be used or areas for further reflection;

f. listen attentively to speaker's summary points, if offered.

Panel Discussion and Forum

The group leader convenes several of the learning group members who have previously acquired specific knowledge on a topic of interest. These persons constitute a panel, and they discuss the topic of interest among themselves in front of the assembled learning group. Immediately after the panel's discussion, there is free and open discussion among the entire group (a forum) in reaction to the panel.

The catechist:

a. chooses three or four learners prior to the session to serve on a panel;

b. prepares a series of questions or reflection statements that members of the panel may use in their preparations and encourages them to research and read on the topic;

c. meets with panel members to help them clarify new learnings and prepare their discussion process;

d. prepares a proper learning environment, situating the panel before all in attendance;

e. introduces the group to the panel members and to the topic to be discussed;

f. facilitates the panel discussion by asking questions, seeking active participation by all panel participants, but does not add personally-held opinions;

g. clarifies content and issues when necessary;

h. focuses on chief insights to be drawn from panel members;

i. encourages all learners to ask questions of panel members or contribute their comments;

j. summarizes key contributions from all involved.

The panel members:

a. consult with the catechist prior to the panel session in order to prepare their parts in the experience;

b. read and research adequately on the topic of interest;

c. contribute during the panel discussion;

d. react to or build upon contributions by other panelists;

e. interact with those who question and comment from the larger group.

The learning group participants:

a. should understand the purpose and direction of the panel activity;

b. seriously listen to and consider the ideas shared by panelists;

c. prepare questions and comments to ask panel members when invited to do so;

d. participate in the full-group forum;

e. help catechist summarize key insights and contributions which have surfaced during the panel and the forum.

Reaction Statements

The group leader prepares a thought-provoking statement which is related to the subject matter at hand. The statement should be directly applicable to the learners' interests and life situations. It should likewise allow for a variety of reactions.

The catechist:

a. prepares the reaction statement, writing it on a handout master;

b. duplicates one copy of the statement for each learner;

c. asks learners to write their reactions to the statement, saying whether they agree or disagree, and why;

d. discussion among participants and then catechist and the full group ensues.

The learners:

a. react individually, in writing, to the statement;

b. contribute their statements verbally in the large group if willing to do so;

c. participate in small group discussions or large group discussions to compare individual reactions;

d. help catechist identify key learnings arising from this activity.

Research and Report

The group leader proposes a specific issue or question to the learning group. Individual members accept responsibility to research certain topics and to share their findings later with the full group, thus building up the knowledge and insight of all involved.

The catechist:

a. assigns issue or questions for research, or helps some group members to select them;

b. helps group members decide upon types of research that will be desired;

c. seeks several learners to do the research voluntarily;

d. identifies (and perhaps furnishes) selected resources from which research can be drawn;

e. calls for reports from those who have completed the research;

f. encourages comments, questions, and reactions from other learners;

g. pinpoints key insights or new directions which have arisen from the research or the ensuing discussions;

h. suggests ways new information could be used by individuals and the whole group.

The learners:

a. if possible, define the issue(s) or question(s) for research along with the leader;

b. seek volunteers who will undertake the research and the reports;

c. support and encourage the researchers;

d. listen attentively to the data presented by the researchers;

e. comment on or question the reports;

f. help identify how new information can be put to good use.

Role-Playing

The group leader proposes a problem-situation; several different learners take on character roles and briefly act out the situation. The phases of an effective role-play are:

1. clearly define the situation;

2. have learners assume the character that will be involved;

3. have characters act out the situation;

4. stop the action before the role-play is exhausted;

5. discuss and evaluate how it went, naming central turning points and outcomes in the role-play.

The catechist:

a. selects the scene for the role-play, or works with some learners to define the problem-situation or issue to consider;

b. identifies roles to be enacted and all other circumstances for the experience;

c. sees that members of the learning group take on various character roles;

d. prepares the full group adequately;

e. gives role-play participants time to prepare away from full group;

f. ends the role-play before action is exhausted;

g. facilitates an analysis and discussion of the role-play among all involved;

h. asks for insights and feedback in particular from role-players;

i. identifies chief issues, new learnings, and/or new directions suggested in the experience;

j. gives input on how new learnings may be further studied or perhaps acted on.

Those taking on character roles:

a. agree to take on the parts (Ideally, each person agrees to a role significantly different from the way he or she is usually perceived by others.);

b. attempt to identify with the viewpoints and feelings of their various characters;

c. develop the action and sequence of events for the role-play;

d. enact the role play;

e. return to their normal personalities when the role-play concludes;

f. help discuss and analyze the words, behaviors, and feelings of the characters in the role-play;

g. offer input on new learnings, chief issues, and new directions surfaced;

h. contribute suggestions on how new insights might be further studied or acted on.

The learning group members:

a. participate (if invited) in setting the scene and selecting key problem/issue to be probed in the role-play;

b. seek clarity from the leader/catechist on the facts of and the process for the activity;

c. observe the role-play;

d. reflect carefully on the problem or issue presented;

e. comment on and question the words and action included in the role-play;

f. participate in discussion on new learnings, new issues, or new directions revealed;

g. consider and comment on how these could be further studied or put into action.

Storytelling

[For additional suggestions on using the storytelling process with music and video presentations, see "Storytelling with Rock Music/Video" later in this chapter.]

Storytelling Strategy #1

The storytelling process can help learners focus on their life experience or reflect their life experience with a story from the life of another, from contemporary music and video, from contemporary films, or from literature.

A step-by-step approach to storytelling follows and begins with a story that can be related to the hearers' experience:

a. tell a story (or play the song, show the video, or show the film) then, select a story which will relate directly to the interests, concerns, and experiences of the hearers;

b. give each group member a chance to share feelings when the story ends;

c. challenge each participant to get in touch with an experience that the story/film/song/video has recalled;

d. invite each member of the group to share a story with others (in small groups, or in the larger group of eight or less);

e. call participants to quiet reflection on the personal insights that have surfaced in this process;

f. invite learners now to individually attempt to recall something about Jesus, or another major figure in our religious tradition (part of his story, an experience from Jesus' life) that resonates with their stories and gives meaning to their stories;

g. ask learners to name/share the Jesus stories they have recalled;

h. challenge them to identify in their groups the religious meaning of this experience and encourage them to speak about how God has been active in their lives

i. discuss the implications of their religious insights for their lives and how will they now change or live differently.

Storytelling Strategy #2

This storytelling process does *not* presume that learners are deeply familiar with the elements of Jesus' story. Thus, it starts with a story about him and, then, helps participants relate some of their personal life experiences to the Jesus event.

a. tell a story about Jesus (through a gospel passage, a song, a video, a storybook, etc.) then, choose a story that will connect directly with the concerns, interests, and hopes of the hearers;

b. ask each group member a chance to share feelings as the story concludes;

c. challenge learners to name the character in the story with whom they most identified, and why;

d. ask participants (again, these steps can occur in smaller groups, or in a larger group of eight or less) to share what significance they found in the story;

e. encourage all to discuss the chief insights they gained about Jesus' mission and ministry;

f. urge each participant to identify a life experience he or she has had that has been recalled through the Jesus story and, if desired, ask them to write their reflections on this life experience;

g. invite all to share their personal experiences with other learners;

h. encourage them to name chief insights they have gained in linking personal experiences with the Jesus story;

i. challenge all to reflect on and discuss the implications of these religious insights for their lives and how will they now change personally or life differently.

Thought Sheet

In using this technique, the catechist is challenging learners to think about and state explicitly their ideas and viewpoints about an element of religious content. The group leader poses a clear, simple question to which learners respond in writing (in the form of a sentence, a paragraph, a couplet, poetry, or a song lyric).

For example, the catechist could pause in the midst of a verbal presentation (one or more times), to ask "What do you think about what was just said about _____ "? or "Why do you suppose that we believe _____ ? Do you agree or disagree with this viewpoint"? Learners could be challenged to write a brief response to each thought-starter question, or challenged to compose a poem or lyric later in response. Discussion on the learners' various thoughts and reactions often ensues.

Work Groups

The group leader helps learners to divide into small group units in order that they can accomplish one or more tasks.

The catechist:

a. sets the task(s) to be accomplished, or does so with the assistance of some learning group members;

b. can assign the identical task to all small groups, or can ask small groups to focus on separate tasks;

c. provides information and resources necessary for groups to do their work;

d. provides clear directions, timelines, and expectations to the small groups;

e. circulates among these work groups to support, encourage, and assist;

f. re-assembles all into larger group;

g. facilitates reporting by groups on results of their work;

h. facilitates discussion among all learners on the whole experience and on results from small groups;

i. identifies key outcomes and new learnings;

j. mentions ways these outcomes could be further studied or acted on.

The small group members:

a. if possible, help define the task(s) for the working groups;

b. pay attention to the directions, guidelines, and expectations provided by the leader;

c. participate fully in achieving the work group's task(s);

d. help prepare and give the report on the working groups' results;

e. participate in the wider discussion on the task(s) and results accomplished by all;

f. help name key outcomes and new learnings;

g. help name ways these could be further studied or put into action;

Audio-Visual Media

As noted earlier, individuals can learn in many ways. Some learn well when verbal activities alone are used (lecture, reading aloud, listening to an audio-cassette); yet, most benefit more as learners when verbal and visual (hearing-and-seeing) activities are complemented in a learning situation. Our religious education has largely centered on the printed and spoken word. Young people who could read well, who were highly verbal, or who remembered things easily were active participants in the catechetical process. Those who were less able to use and understand words, printed or spoken, did not fare so well. Catechists in recent years have endeavored to provide a wider variety of learning methods and educational techniques to reach all learners, including an increased use of various audio-visual learning activities.

We are rediscovering, therefore, that visual and artistic presentations can communicate much religious meaning. Learners can be communicated with through various media: rock music and rock video as mentioned previously, plus films, full-length movie video-cassettes, filmstrips, slides, audio-cassette tapes, overhead projectors, and others. Incidentally, it is also quite possible for young learners to communicate religiously with us through these audio-visual methods, or to communicate religiously and meaningfully with each other, when given the chance to create their own media presentations.

In his book, *Using Media in Religious Education,* Ronald A. Sarno says,

> The Christian church, like the rest of the modern world, is being rapidly altered because of an unprecedented global alteration in the world's information-environment. Since 1950 the principal communication tool for connecting people with their world has radically shifted from the printed text of the literate culture to the . . . image-amplified sound of the audiovisual culture.[4]

Thus, religious educators must understand and accept a changing situation. People accustomed to audiovisual entertainment as a way of life tend to evaluate information and changes (sometimes critically, but often uncritically) based on how meaningful they are to their *present* experience. Often, to those raised in our "audiovisual culture," the printed text can merely symbolize the irrelevant *past,* rather than the present or the future. Catechists must begin to see their efforts as a form of communication, an element of the new, global "information-environment." We should recognize more fully that learners can and will thoroughly benefit from the use of amplified sound-and-images. Members of our young media-generation will be more actively engaged in the total learning process when sight-and-sound techniques are used in conjunction with printed and spoken words. In incorporating various contemporary media into our catechesis, we help make our Catholic tradition more relevant, present, and alive for the youth in our Church.

Here are some suggested questions to use in actually selecting audio-visual media for catechetical events:

- Does this A-V help learners better understand the subject? Does it provide clear, essential information in an interesting way?

- Is this A-V appropriate for the age group(s) with which it will be used?

- Is this A-V so unusual, novel, or striking that its real value will be lost to the group?

- Is this A-V enjoyable enough that seeing-and-hearing it will give the learners a sense of accomplishment and satisfaction?

- Is this A-V accompanied by guidelines or creative suggestions on how to use it with your learning group?

- Is this resource brand new, or has it been used successfully by others? How has it been used?

- Does this A-V center learners' attention on important issues, questions, or role models which they should reflect on carefully?

- Will this A-V challenge learners to reflect critically, or imaginatively and creatively think about possibilities?

- Is this A-V one that urges learners to study further or to act on their insights?

- Will this A-V bore or frustrate the learners?

- Does this A-V suggest connections between its main theme/content and the gospel of Jesus?

Audio-Visual Methods

Films: 16 MM

a. In catechetical situations, films should *not* be used as time-fillers, entertainment only, lecture substitutes, nor before being thoroughly previewed by the catechist(s) involved.

b. Before showing the film to a group, start learners off with one or two focus questions to think about during the film.

c. After viewing the film, have the learners discuss:
  — How did the film make you feel?
  — What were the most memorable scenes or images?
  — Which of the characters seems most interesting to you? Were there conflicts?
  — What was this film all about? What did it say or teach? (could be one, two, or many things)
  — Discuss the focus question(s);
  — have each person answer: What insight or new learning have you gotten from this film? How will you apply this to your daily life as a Christian?

d. Films can be interrupted at times so that the leader can check out viewers' comments and reactions to the story; focus questions can also be initially discussed during these times.

Video-Cassette (Hollywood) Movies

a. all that was said above regarding 16mm films can apply here, including the suggested discussion process;

b. preview and writing of focus questions should occur with catechist(s) and several learning group members combining their efforts whenever possible.

Filmstrips

a. introduce the group to the central topic/theme and some key ideas to be found in the filmstrip presentation;

b. provide one or two focus questions for the learners to reflect n during their viewing;

c. show the whole filmstrip, or show it in parts, with brief discussions occurring between the parts shown

d. follow the viewing with some reflections on:
— How did this A-V make you feel?
— What pictures, symbols, or spoken words really stood out? how did the soundtrack music (if any) affect you?
— What chief ideas did the filmstrip's makers hope to get across?
— What main idea(s) did you get? what did you learn from it?
— Discuss then the focus question(s)
— How will you use the insights you received from this filmstrip in your daily life?

Slide/Sound Presentations

Adolescent catechesis has engaged young people in creating their own slide/sound presentations in recent years. Here are some basic guidelines.

● Why have students create a slide-and-sound presentation?

● They will examine elements of the gospel or their wider faith tradition.

● Their catechist(s) will be able to spend some extra hours with the learners helping them in a special way with the A-V project.

● In examining their faith more closely, learners may also choose to live it and share it with others more thoroughly.

● Those learners interested more in media, photography, artwork, community-experiences, and technical work, than in the same-old religious education, may find this interesting and motivating.

● Linking contemporary rock music to the gospel and religion may cause them to more closely analyze what they hear and see in rock'n roll every day.

● Finding appropriate scenes and pictures for slides will help them recognize how that which they ordinarily see and encounter has a truly religious dimension.

● The final product (a slide-and-sound show on a religious topic) could help build lines of greater communication and understanding between its creators and those to whom it is shown.

How to help youth prepare a slide-and-sound presentation:

a. Select a main topic or theme ("the sayings of Jesus" or "our parish is a faith community"). Write a script consisting of 20-30 items or messages (20 things the gospels say Christ said, or 25 sentences that stress ways the parish acts as a faithful body of people).

b. Have some group members take original pictures to be made into slides; others can borrow pictures/slides from families, other parishioners; others can search through slides that the diocesan audio-visual center might own.

c. Some group members match the elements of the script with the slides available (these learners should be encouraged to use their imaginations).

d. After script and slides have been matched up, learners should select opening and closing musical selections, plus the music during the times that slides-and-script are presented. These accompanying music sounds should never intrude on the central importance of the script.

e. The group members should also write an effective introduction and conclusion to the entire presentation.

f. Write invitations to other groups (e.g., parents, parish leadership, CCD classes, younger students in school, etc.) asking them to attend your slide-and-sound presentation at a certain time and place.

g. Prepare the environment for the presentation (including the types of hospitality to be offered); obtain the needed equipment; have some learners volunteer to clean-up and put away materials used when the presentation ends.

Television and Radio Commercials

For specific suggestions on how to watch and critically reflect on these forms of media with young Christians, see the "Youth Culture: Consumerism and Youth" section of the *Enablement Resource Manual*. Several processes for raising consumer awareness and media literacy among adolescents are included there.

Discussing a Rock Song

Form your group/class into small groups of three-six persons each. Introduce the song, the name(s) of the performer(s), and show the album from which it comes. If you like, have a person in the group read or recite the lyrics of the piece. Or you could display the song's words on an overhead transparency as the music plays. Sources that give out lyrics to contemporary songs are identified below. Then,

a. Play the song (kind of loud, as rock's supposed to be);

b. After the group(s) have heard it, begin the discussion here:

— How does this song make you feel (e.g., happy, sad, glad, afraid, angry, hopeful, confused, ready to party)?

— Did you like it? Why? Why not? What was the beat like? What special sounds (effects) did you like? (Note: these are sometimes called "hooks.")

— What was the "message" or main point in the song? (You may want to re-play it here, or simply re-read the lyrics with all.)

c. Have each small group make a report to all on the various "messages" heard.

— What was the picture of relationships between people that came through? What was the outlook on woman? What was the outlook on man?

— Is this the kind of song/album/performers that we Christians can "buy" (as in agree with, believe in)? Should a Christian spend time or money on such a song/ artist? Why, why not?

— Do you think this song/performer(s) is urging you to do or believe something through this rock song? Is that in line with what Jesus and his gospel values call for from us?

d. Have small groups give reports to all now on these final questions.

Summarize the major ideas and insights heard from the small groups using the rock themes outline below. Explain how the main "messages" in the song (and as seemingly embodied by its performer) either fit in line with gospel values and Church teaching, or diverge from them.

1. **Main Message**
   These songs are proclamations about having fun and good times, partying, holding on to youth, cutting loose. In these, the idea can be genuine, meaningful recreation (in a positive sense). Such songs are celebrative, upbeat, full of hope. Or in these, the idea can be more along the lines of party–ing and escaping in an irresponsible or rebellious fashion.

2. **Songs about Relationships**
   For example:
   a. On Youth Community, Families, Friendships. Such music expresses desires for belonging, friendship, genuine communication.
   b. On Sex, Love, and Falling Out of Love. Surely about four of every five rock pieces focus on these topics. Some songs here are thoughtful, heartfelt, and sensitive, even saddening. Yet too often, sex is imaged as a means for quick satisfaction; women come across as mere objects of desire, and relationships are depicted as temporary, little-consequence affairs.

3. **Songs on Social Problems**
   Social problem songs entertain, but also disturb us somehow—that is rock music tension at its best! A common theme herein is: something has gone awry in our modern world.

4. Songs about Escape/Running Away

For example:

a. Into Chemical/Substance Abuse. A few songs focus on avoiding or denying reality through alcohol, dry drugs, or addictive relationships.

b. Running Away, or Hitting the Open Road. A classic American loner myth. When the pinch is on, the going gets rough, he or she leaves it all behind to get some space.

5. Songs about Inner Pressures

In our society, stresses build up, the internal life gets heavier. These songs ponder those pressures. Some even express fears that life is getting "out of control."

6. Facing an Unsure Future

We all wonder now and then, especially those young people worried about what kind of future they will have. Some of these songs express big fears and questions. Now and then they urge hope and constructive risk. Strongly religious themes will surface in some of these pieces also.

Finish your group discussion with final youth contributions. Thank all for sharing in open-minded ways. Close with a prayer, and Aretha Franklin's song, "I Knew You Were Waiting For Me" (LP: *Aretha,* Arista Records, 1986), or The Call's, "Everywhere I Go" (LP: *Reconciled*). Use other reflective, prayerful songs when using this group process at future times.

Discussing a Rock Video

Begin this in the same way we did with "Discussing a Rock Song" above. However, play the song first (without the video), as above, then show the video clip. Then pick up with the discussion process:

— What were you feeling like as this video ended (e.g., share genuine feelings—happy, mad, depressed, confused, hopeful, anxious, etc.)?

— What was "the story" in the video, if it had one?

— Which were the most memorable, wild, or eye-catching images/scenes? (Discuss the meaning of each...)

Use small group, check-in reports here.

— What was the bottom-line point or message of the video to you? (Some may think it didn't have any.)

— Every rock video clip is on-purpose, designed to "sell" something to us. What thing(s) was this one selling (e.g,, performers, their values, point of view, a product—such as a movie or a concert tour, an album)?

— How do you suppose Jesus would have reacted if he were here watching this with us? Please explain . . . .

Seek small group reports here on each of the chief questions above.

— Any other thoughts or questions now?

As group leader/catechist, finish this process in the same way you would for "Discussing a Rock Song."

The Thoughtful Listener Worksheet

Form your class/group into about three or four subunits. (Each unit should be assigned to focus on only one song.) Play three or four contemporary "radio chart" hits for all, one at a time. (Get volunteers to help you pick these beforehand.) Display the lyrics for each song as it plays. Then, as individual subunits, have your members use the following questions (printed for all on a work-sheet) to discuss the one song their unit has been assigned:

1. Did you like this rock song? Why, why not?
2. What was the best part in the words?
3. What kind of reputation does this singer/ group have?
4. What would your parents say about this song?
5. What do your friends say about it?
6. What do your Catholic beliefs tell you to think about this song? this performer/group?
7. If Jesus came here to listen to records with us, which of these 3 or 4 songs should we play for him? Which should we leave out? Explain please....

Have subunit reporters give brief reports for the other youth. Before each report, you might re-play the song the sub-group considered. Obviously, with minor modifications you can use this worksheet outline with video clips, rather than music only.

Dial-a-Rock Star Interview

Use this technique as a listening (and role-play) activity with your kids. Listen to rock 'n roll songs with a strong message, either positive or negative. (You could also view the song's video, if it is appropriate.)

Use a selection of the discussion questions provided by the activities above. Then, view and comment, with the whole group, on the album cover (from which the song comes) and maybe pictures/posters of the performer or group.

Then ask your group members to fill-in a phone interview sheet, pretending they're having individual telephone conversations.

Share these, either by reading aloud or by role-playing phone conversations with a phone prop, in the large group/class. Close with the "rock art" process included in the "Heavy Metal" section below.

Rock and the Good Life

Ask your group/class members to bring one rock music thing (a song, album, poster, video, concert booklet, T-shirt, interview, lyric, etc.) that says something to each about what it means to live a "good life." (*Note:* You should review these before the session begins to avoid unpleasant shocks or surprises.) In sharing circles (six-eight persons or less), ask them to share in these areas: (You should circulate among groups as this goes on.)
— This is what I brought in . . . It's most important to me because . . .
— The way that this really challenges me to grow up is . . .
— It helps me as a Christian (or it holds me back some) in that it . . .

Thank all for their cooperation and sharing. As the catechist, you could summarize chief points you've heard/observed in circulating among the small groups. [Also, you could point out key ideas in my essay, "Notes On Consumerism Among American Teenagers," which is included in the *Enablement Resource Manual.*] Discuss these with all.

Close with a prayerful song. You could have all join hands and offer spontaneous prayers too, if your learners can handle such prayer activity.

Dial-a-Rock Star Interview	
Date: _____	Time: _____

You: _____

Rocker: _____

You: _____

Rocker: _____

You: _____

Rocker: _____

You: _____

Rocker: _____

You: _____

Heavy Metal Rock Activity

Plan to do a heavy metal discussion with your group. To prepare:

1. For several days, use a VCR to record MTV's daily, afternoon heavy metal show (3:30 P.M. EST). Select a few good videos and interview segments to use;

2. Preview and reflect on current heavy metal rock videos you can use ("Twilight Hotel" by Quiet Riot; "Wasted Years" or "Stranger In a Strange Land" by Iron Maiden; "Peace Sells, But Who's Buying" by Megadeath; "Calling On You" by Stryper; "Talk Dirty To Me" by Poison). Quite a few heavy metal acts have video collections on full-length cassettes, such as "Uncensored" by Motley Crue (on Elektra Video). You could rent these from a local video-rental store;

3. Select a couple Celebrity profiles/interviews from teenager's heavy metal magazines, like *Hit Parader* and *Circus.* Read and discuss with the group;

4. Ask for volunteers to bring in popular album covers, posters, magazines, videos, bumperstickers, T-shirts, and "artwork" from the heavy metal world. (*Note:* You'll want to look these over first before they're shown to the whole group.) Do some general sharing and discussion of the items. Break the group into small working teams of three or four. Pass out newsprint sheets and an assortment of colored markers.

Ask the teams to:
a. list in separate columns the positive and the negative aspects of heavy metal and heavy metal visuals in young people's lives, and
b. draw a Christian-values rock album cover, both the front and the back panels. When they are done, have the teams share their lists and their artistic designs.

[This activity first appeared with "Video Rock Highlights," by Butch Ekstrom, in *Top Music Countdown Journal* (Santa Rosa, CA: Cornerstone Media; Winter 1987 issue). For more information on *TMC*, see the bibliography at the end of this chapter.]

Storytelling with Rock Music/Video—#1
(Try this with older adolescents. It may not be effective with younger adolescents.)

Introduce this experience in much the same way we did in "Discussing a Rock Song" above.

— Play the song (and/or show the video), kind of loud;
— Share how the piece makes each person feel; see the process for "Discussing a Rock Song";
— Ask participants to remember a similar experience they have had that the song/video has stirred up;
— Invite them to share their stories with others (in small groups);
— Ask them: What have you learned from the song/video and your memory/story?
— Ask them: Can you think of a story Jesus told, a time in Jesus' life, or in the life of a Christian, that relates to your own story?
— Share these insights in small groups;
— What have you learned from this music and storytelling overall?
— What are you feeling now? What do you think you should do again/ begin to do now?

Storytelling with Rock Music/Video— #2
(Try this with both younger and older adolescents.)

— Tell a "Jesus story"; use the gospel, a film, a story book, your own wording; make sure adolescents can relate to the episode used;
— Ask all to share genuine feelings they are having; give all a chance to do so (small or large group); it takes some urging;
— Who did you identify with most in this story? What did the story mean to you? Did you learn, or re-learn, something about Jesus?
— Provide background to the gospel story;
— *Option*: in groups, create rock video scripts (that is, identify a song plus images) that "re-write" in contemporary terms the Jesus story;
— Ask all to share these with full class/group;
— What new insights or messages do you get now about Jesus? about really being a Christian?
— What are you feeling now? What do you think you should begin/ continue doing?

Using Negative Rock Songs/Videos

(This design was written by Lynn Mahoney, Youth Minister, St. Francis Xavier Parish, Metarie, Louisiana.) Contrary to popular belief, songs with a negative twist or theme do not often pop up these days on the air waves. However, some artists are determined to pound out their messages even though the values and actions imaged in their songs/videos do not match up with society norms or Christian beliefs. Those of us committed to enabling young people to unlock and interpret rock lyrics/videos should confront these issue songs with the same intensity we approach positive themes. Here is an outline for an evening class with youth that might help.

Arrival and Introduction to Evening (5 minutes)
(Note: Play rock music during this time; pass out name tags.)

Icebreaker (10 minutes)
Invite group members to pair off for this activity. Ask each member of the pair to share answers to the following:

1. Who is your favorite rock recording artist?
2. What is your favorite video currently on the charts?
3. What topics/issues do rock artists sing about these days?
4. What topics/issues do rock artists sing about that concern you or trouble you?

In the large group, invite those who wish to share their responses to do so. (*Note*: Responses to each question could be recorded on separate sheets of newsprint and taped to the wall for future reference.)

Video Viewing (25 minutes)

Show/play two or three rock videos/songs (current or "oldies") that contain negative themes/images. Ask each dyad to join another to form groups of four. After each video/song, invite the groups to answer the following:

1. How does this rock video—its beat, sound, visuals—make you feel?
2. What is the video's main message in both its lyrics and video images? Do the two match up?
3. Can you recall a time when you confronted this issue or came face-to-face with this problem in your life?

Then ask each group to summarize and report their discussion to the larger group.

Poster Activity (30 minutes)
Distribute newsprint or poster board to each group of four. Ask them to create a poster with the following:

This Week's Message To Youth
Video Rock Says . . . (summarize findings from previous video exercise)

Jesus Says . . . (look up gospel passages to support these statements/quotes)

(*Note*: Encourage art work here, too.)

Invite all to display and explain their poster and thank everyone for their hard work and participation.

Closing Prayer (5 minutes)
(Choose a scripture passage used in the "Jesus Says" portion of the poster activity; invite spontaneous prayer.)

Notes

1. Edgar Dale, *Audio-Visual Methods in Teaching* 3rd ed. (New York: Holf, Rinehart and Winston, Inc., 1946, 1954, 1969) p. 42.

2. Ibid, p. 43.

3. Malcolm Knowles, *Modern Practice of Adult Education. (New York: Cambridge Books, 1969) p. 240*.

4. Ronald Sarno, *Using Media* in Religious Education. (Birmingham, AL: Religious Education Process, 1987) p. 35.

Resources on Learning Methods

Clark, Jean Illsely. *Who Me Lead a Group?* San Francisco: Harper and Row, 1984.

Everist, Norma. *Education Ministry in the Congregation*. Minneapolis, MN: Augsburg, 1983.

Griggs, Donald. *Teaching Teachers To Teach.* Nashville, TN: Abingdon Press, 1974.

Griggs, Donald. *Planning for Teaching Church School.* Nashville, TN: Abingdon Press, 1985.

Hyman, Ronald. *Improving Discussion* Leadership. New York: Teachers College Press, 1980.

Knowles, Malcolm and Hulda. *Introduction to Group Dynamics.* New York: Cambridge Books, 1972.

Layman, James. *Using Case Studies in Church Education.* Scottsdale, AZ: National Teacher Education Project, 1977.

LeFever, Marlene. *Creative Teaching Methods.* Elgin, IL: David C. Cook, 1985.

Leypoldt, Martha, *40 Ways to Teach in Groups.* Valley Forge, PA: Judson Press, 1967.

Little, Sara. *Learning Together in the Christian Fellowship.* Richmond, VA: John Knox Press, 1956.

Reichert, Richard. *Simulation Games for Religious Education.* Winona, MN: St. Mary's Press, 1975.

Resources on Rock Music and Rock Video

Printed:

Hibbert, Tom. The *Rock Yearbook 1987.* New York: St. Martin's Press/
    Virgin Books, 1986.

Pareles, Jon and P. Romanowski, editors. *The Rolling Stone Rock 'N Roll
    Encyclopedia.* New York: Rolling Stone Press/Summit Books, 1983).

Shore, Michael. The *Rolling Stone Book of Rock Video.* New York:
    Rolling Stone Press, 1984.

Top Music Countdown—Journal on rock 'n roll for Catholic ministers and
    parents (quarterly). Edited by Rev. Don Kimball. Cornerstone Media, P.
    0. Box 6236, Santa Rosa, CA 95406. Four seasonal issues—$15.00 per
    year. Ask for the practical User's Guide, "Five Basic (Youth) Meetings
    on Rock: Leader Information Sheet," edited by Rev. Don Kimball,
    Cornerstone Media.

Audio Cassettes:

"Dirty Dozen/Psalm 151" (1986 edition, and 1987 edition). Annual review of
    the best and worst rock songs on values from each year by Cornerstone
    Media (as above). $15 each.

"Cornerstone Review Cassettes", a monthly audio-magazine by Fr. Don
    Kimball. 12 cassettes, $140 per year. Includes practical recorded and
    print materials for youth programs. By Cornerstone Media.

"Praying With Our Headphones," 90 minutes on how to build popular music
    into prayer experiences and personal growth exercises, by Cornerstone
    Media. $15.

"Backtalk," two, 90-minute radio call-in shows about Satanic influences in
    rock. From Cornerstone Media. $25.

Wavelength. Youth and Young Adult Ministries, Diocese of Sacramento, 2519
    L St., Sacramento, CA 95816. Monthly Cassette Program and Process
    Guide reviewing rock music and its themes. $75/year.

Chapter 8

Evaluating Adolescent Catechesis

Evaluation is an essential and often forgotten step in adolescent catechesis. *Sharing the Light of Faith,* the National Catechetical Directory (*NCD*), reminds us that planning is essential to every catechetical effort, but adds that program evaluation should always occur too. "Catechetical programs should be subjected to regular evaluations. The evaluation should be made in light of established goals and objectives, which themselves should be evaluated periodically" (*NCD*, #222).

Thomas Walters, in *Handbook for Parish Evaluation,* writes:

> First, program evaluation is not a luxury. Catechetical programs because they are by design intended to make a noticeable difference in people's lives must concern themselves with effectiveness. Did the program accomplish what it set out to do? If a catechetical program is not achieving its intended goal it is ineffective and must be changed.
>
> Second, the purpose of program evaluation is change for the better. Program evaluation is basically a systematic and objective process which compares *what the program intended to do* with *what the program actually accomplished, to determine how the program can be improved.*[1]

Program evaluation needs to be a regularly scheduled process. At the completion of a faith theme learning plan, a season, semester or quarter, and the entire year, evaluations should be conducted. The young people, the catechists/religion teachers, coordinators and administrators, should all be involved in evaluation. There are several steps to creating your evaluation process:

1. Formulate the criteria for the areas you want to evaluate;

2. Formulate the questions you want answered;

3. Collect the data that will help you answer these questions;

4. Analyze this data and interpret the answers it holds for the key questions;

5. Develop recommendations to modify, change, improve and strengthen your goals, programs, procedures, and vision in light of your findings;

6. Use your recommendations by returning to the curriculum development process (Chapter 3 in this Manual) and plan your next year or season of programming by beginning with Step #5 — designing the learning plan for each faith theme.

Is the catechetical evaluation process really worth the time and effort? Is it more trouble than it is good news? What can it really accomplish? Yes! An evaluation can provide affirmation and legitimation for your efforts, thereby giving the adolescent catechesis program solid backing in the parish or school. Second, through an evaluation a catechetical program can be altered. Learning plans and objectives can be reviewed and redefined. New needs and new interests among youth and their parents can come to light and be addressed. The overall operation of the program can be strengthened and even streamlined.

Following the evaluation of a catechetical program, the results and findings should be reported to all who participate in the process, and to all the others interested in or involved in the program. These findings should give details about the decisions that program leaders have made and describe the actions that have been taken following the evaluation process.

Finally, it is quite likely that among recommendations and ideas which come out of an evaluation, the majority will relate directly to improvements in individual courses or learning activities. Therefore, the catechetical coordinators should share, completely and honestly, with catechists the judgments and suggestions that have been made about the teachings activities for which they are responsible. These judgments and suggestions should be presented before staff members as things to celebrate and enjoy, as well as objective problems to solved. They should not be presented as personal indictments, so that constructive action can build upon these evaluation findings.

To assist you in designing your evaluation process you will find five model evaluation forms in this chapter. Be sure to adapt these for your particular situation. [*Note:* Permission is granted to photocopy these evaluation forms.]

For Further Resources on Evaluation

Walters, Thomas (editor). *Handbook For Parish Evaluation.* New Jersey: Paulist Press, 1984.

Note

1. Thomas Walters ed. *Handbook For Parish Evaluation.* (New Jersey: Paulist Press, 1984) p. 5.

Evaluation Instrument #1:

Evaluating a Faith Theme

Using the format of the faith themes learning plan, you can evaluate each theme through the following questions. You can take these questions and create your own evaluation forms for your catechists/teachers, adolescent catechesis team/committee, religious education board, and the catechetical coordinators.

A. Needs and Interests

1. What particular needs/interests of adolescents did this faith theme address? (If you conducted a needs assessment, what needs did this theme respond to?) What did the young people expect to get out of this learning experience?

2. In what specific ways did this faith theme address their needs/interests.

B. Learning Objectives

1. What learning objectives did you develop for this faith theme? How did they focus on the three dimensions of Christian faith: Trusting, Believing, Doing?

2. To what extent were you able to realize the learning objectives? Be specific.

3. In view of your experience, how would you alter these objectives for the future?

C. Learning Model, Setting, and Schedule

1. How effective was the learning model for this faith theme? What was the response of the young people to the learning model? What is your assessment of this model? What changes might you make in the model?

2. How conducive was the setting to learning? What was the response of the young people to the setting? What changes might you make in the setting?

3. How effective was the schedule (dates, times, number of sessions) for teaching this faith theme, in promoting participation of young people in the faith theme? What changes might you make in the scheduling?

D. Methods and Content

1. Describe briefly the principal methods you employed in this faith theme.

2. To which of these did the young people respond best?

3. Describe briefly the material covered in this activity.

4. What material did the young people respond best?

5. Appraise the interest of the participants in this faith theme (methods and content)? Did it fluctuate significantly? (If so, can you cite specific causes?)

6. What suggestions for improvement (methods and content) can you make?

E. Overall Evaluation

1. To what extent do you feel this learning experience fulfilled its objectives?

2. What specific results were accomplished with individuals? What changes in thinking, feeling, and acting took place? (Cite cases.)

3. What general recommendations would you make for the improvement of this faith theme?

Evaluation Instrument #2:

Evaluating Courses

Use the following four forms to design your own course evaluation.

Course Evaluation #1

Please respond to the following items by noting your feelings and/or thoughts about the statements listed.

1. As a this course (circle the number that best describes your thoughts):

   a. I am more confident of _____

Strongly Disagree		Mildly Disagree		Mildly Agree	Strongly Agree
1	2	3	4	5	6

   b. I can apply this knowledge to _____

SD		MD		MA	SA
1	2	3	4	5	6

   c. I feel my time has been well spent.

SD		MD		MA	SA
1	2	3	4	5	6

2. List three specific ways in which this course has deepened your faith:

3. List three ways in which you can apply your learning to your life:

4. The teacher shows (circle the number that best describes your judgment):

   a. Knowledge of the content of the course.

SD		MD		MA	SA
1	2	3.	4	5	6

   b. An ability to create a learning atmosphere.

SD		MD		MA	SA
1	2	3	4	5	6

   c. Creativity in teaching style, methods, and techniques.

SD		MD		MA	SA
1	2	3	4	5	6

d. An ability to involve participants in the learning experience.

SD	MD		MA		SA
1	2	3	4	5	6

e. A willingness to share own personal faith and life experiences openly.

SD	MD		MA		SA
1	2	3	4	5	6

5. Please rate each of the course topics. (1 = Not; 5 = Very) (You can use any number of indicators—interesting, enriching, helpful, etc.)

a. _____ 1 2 3 4 5

6. Additional comments and/or recommendations:

_____

_____

_____

Course Evaluation #2

1. I feel this session was (circle one):

very helpful   somewhat helpful   not very helpful   not helpful

2. I was please by/with:

_____

_____

_____

3. I was disappointed or dissatisfied by/with:

_____

_____

_____

4. I learned:

_____

_____

_____

Course Evaluation #3

1. What is your overall feeling after participating in this course?
   [Circle the one(s) that most apply.]

   Enthused   Astounded   Satisfied   Indifferent   Angry
   Ambivalent   Irritated   Uneasy   Threatened   Discouraged

2. What did you hope to gain from participating in this course?

   _____

   _____

   _____

3. How well were your expectations fulfilled? [Check one.]

   _____ Completely _____ Mostly _____ Partially _____ Not at all

4. How do you feel about the amount of presentation and the amount of activities/
   discussion in this session? [Check one.]

   _____ Too much presentation _____ Too much discussion _____ A good mixture

5. Benefits and learnings that I gained from this course include:

   _____

   _____

   _____

6. Disappointments and dissatisfactions I experienced in this course include:

   _____

   _____

   _____

7. How do you rate the physical facilities?

   _____ Fine _____ Good _____ Okay _____ Poor

8. How do you rate the scheduling and length of the course?

   _____ Fine _____ Good _____ Okay _____ Poor

9. Some suggestions I'd like to make to improve this course:

   _____

   _____

   _____

Course Evaluation #4

Name of Course _____

Teacher _____

Please answer the following questions as honestly as possible. This will help us to make this an even better course for the others next semester.

1. What did you like the most about this course?

   _____

   _____

2. What did you like the least about this course?

   _____

   _____

3. Did this course help you to grow in Christian values?

   Greatly   Somewhat   None

	(Circle one)			
Poor				Excellent

4. Did the program satisfy your learning needs?   1   2   3   4   5

5. What is your opinion of the program content?   1   2   3   4   5

6. What is your opinion of the presentation?   1   2   3   4   5

7. How would you rate your teacher?   1   2   3   4   5

8. Would you recommend this course to other youth? _____ Yes _____ No

9. In giving your opinion of this course to others would you say it was . . . (Circle one).

   Good   OK   Boring

10. What course would you like to see us offer next semester?

    _____

    Any additional comments you have would be appreciated.

Evaluation Instrument #3:

Evaluating the Program With Staff, Parish/School Leaders, and/or Parents

Date: _____

1. What are some of the strengths of our adolescent catechesis program?

   a. _____

   b. _____

2. What are some of the apparent weaknesses of our adolescent catechesis program?

   a. _____

   b. _____

3. For the coming year, what should you try to do more of, or concentrate on, in order to strengthen the program?

4. For the coming, what specific changes should we make in this ministry?

5. How do you rate the types of printed materials we currently use in our adolescent catechesis program (textbooks, teacher guides, handouts)?

1	2	3	4	5	6	7	8
ineffective			effective			very effective	

6. How do you rate the various audio-visual resources that we currently use (e.g. films, videos, music, slides, filmstrips)?

1	2	3	4	5	6	7	8
ineffective			effective			very effective	

7. Effective adolescent catechesis builds upon the needs and readiness of the young person (intellectual, emotional, social, moral, faith needs). How effective is our program in building upon youth's needs and "readiness" for what is presented?

1	2	3	4	5	6	7	8
ineffective			effective			very effective	

8. Adolescent catechesis attempts to sponsor and guide young people toward maturity in faith. How do we rate in efforts to do this?

1	2	3	4	5	6	7	8
ineffective			effective			very effective	

9. Is there enough parent/family involvement in our adolescent catechesis program?

_____ Yes _____ No _____ Unsure

Suggestions for improving this aspect of your program?

_____

_____

_____

_____

10. Is there significant involvement of and support from the wider faith community for our adolescent catechesis program?

_____ Yes _____ No _____ Unsure

Suggestions for improving this aspect of your program?

_____

_____

_____

_____

11. Please give one specific response to each of the following. In our adolescent catechesis program:

- We help youth learn the message of Jesus and the teachings of the Church through our. . . .
- We help youth build and experience Christian community through our . . .
- We help youth experience prayer and worship through . . .
- We help youth serve (reach out to) others in need through . . .
- We could improve our efforts by . . .

12. What signs do you observe among our youth, or within our wider faith community, that indicate our adolescent catechesis program is having a positive effect?

_____

_____

_____

_____

Thank you for completing this evaluation. Your time and insights are much appreciated.

Evaluation Instrument #4:

Evaluating the Program With the Religious Education Board, DRE, Pastor, Adolescent Catechesis Coordinator, Coordinator of Youth Ministry; Religion Department Chairperson, Principal

Please take a few minutes to complete this evaluation instrument. Then bring it our to meeting to evaluate adolescent catechesis in our parish/school. This meeting will take place on (date) from (time) till (time). Your cooperation and help will be much appreciated. Looking forward to your input at this important meeting.

Date _____

1. Do the leaders and staff for our adolescent catechesis program(s) witness to gospel values and a sense of Christian mission?

_____ Yes _____ No _____ Unsure

Please explain:

_____

_____

_____

2. Is our adolescent catechesis program adequately staffed?

_____ Yes _____ No _____ Unsure

Please explain:

_____

_____

_____

3. Do the leaders and staff of our adolescent catechesis program(s) foster a sense of prayer and community among participants?

_____ Yes _____ No _____ Unsure

Please explain:

_____

_____

_____

4. Do adolescent catechesis leaders work effectively with the appropriate committees and others to plan, implement, and promote adolescent catechesis in the community?

_____ Yes _____ No _____ Unsure

Please explain:

_____

_____

5. How effective is the administrative work of our adolescent catechesis coordinator(s)/ director(s) (e.g. planning programs, organizing staffing, record-keeping, communication)?

1	2	3	4	5	6	7	8
ineffective			effective			very effective	

Please explain:

_____

_____

6. Is there adequate parent/family involvement in our adolescent catechesis program(s)?

_____ Yes _____ No _____ Unsure

Please explain:

_____

_____

7. How do you rate our present efforts to communicate with the parents of our learners?

1	2	3	4	5	6	7	8
ineffective			effective			very effective	

Please explain:

_____

_____

8. The particular strengths of our catechetical program with younger adolescents:

a. _____

b. _____

Suggestions for improvement:

_____

9. The particular strengths of our catechetical program with older adolescents:

a. _____

b. _____

Suggestions for improvement:

_____

_____

10. The weaknesses of our programs (be specific):

a. _____

b. _____

11. Do the staff members of the adolescent catechesis program(s) presently receive adequate training, encouragement, and support for their ministry?

_____ Yes _____ No _____ Unsure

Please explain:

_____

_____

_____

12. Are the printed resources, facilities, and times we currently use suitable for reaching our goals in adolescent catechesis?

_____ Yes _____ No _____ Unsure

Specific suggestions:

_____

_____

_____

13. Please give one specific response to each of the following. In our adolescent catechesis program:

- We help youth learn the message of Jesus and the teachings of the Church through our. . . .
- We help youth build and experience Christian community through our . . .
- We help youth experience prayer and worship through . . .
- We help youth serve (reach out to) others in need through . . .
- We could improve our efforts by . . .

14. Other comments about adolescent catechesis in our community:

Thank you for completing this evaluation. Your time and insights are much appreciated.

Evaluation Instrument #5:

Evaluating the Program With Catechists/ Teachers and Aides

Please complete the following evaluation based upon your experiences in our adolescent catechesis program and on your hopes and goals for future years.

Date _____

Level(s) which you teach: _____

Topics/subject matter which are address:

1. What did youth learn from our adolescent catechesis programs, as whole, during the past year?

   _____

2. What are some key things you think they learned in the course you taught with them (understanding, attitudes, lifestyle)?

   _____

3. What had you hoped they would learn that apparently they did not?

   _____

4. What are the strengths of our adolescent catechesis program(s)?

   a. _____

   b. _____

5. What are its most obvious weaknesses?

   a. _____

   b. _____

6. What should we concentrate on more or do more of, to strengthen this ministry? (Be specific)

   _____

7. How do you rate the printed materials we currently use (textbooks, teacher guides, handouts)?

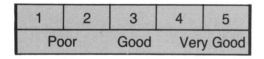

1	2	3	4	5
Poor		Good		Very Good

8. How do you rate the audio-visuals that we use (e.g. films, videos, music, filmstrips)?

1	2	3	4	5
Poor		Good		Very Good

9. Any specific suggestions on how to improve our printed or audio-visual materials?

_____

_____

10. Adolescent catechesis attempts to sponsor and guide young people toward maturity in faith. How do you rate our program's efforts to do this? (choose one or two items)

not effective _____   getting better _____

effective with many youth _____   very effective _____

Comments:

_____

_____

11. Please give one specific response to each of the following. In our adolescent catechesis program:
- We help youth learn the message of Jesus and the teachings of the Church through our. . . .
- We help youth build and experience Christian community through our . . .
- We help youth experience prayer and worship through . . .
- We help youth serve (reach out to) others in need through . . .
- We could improve our efforts by . . .

12. Other ways you observe young people growing in faith within our wider faith community:

_____

13. Other comments about our ministry of adolescent catechesis":

_____

14. What are your hopes/goals as a catechist/teacher for the coming year?

_____

_____

Thank you for completing this evaluation. Your time and insights are much appreciated.

Recognizing the diversity in theologies, ages, and pastoral practices of the sacrament of Confirmation, *The Challenge* tried to offer a context for viewing Confirmation preparation within adolescent catechesis. The trend toward high school Confirmation began in the 1970s. Today the vast majority of dioceses in the United States confirm in the high school years with sophomore and junior years the most popular. While the theological underpinning for Confirmation as a distinct sacrament celebrated in the high school years (and out of sequence and context from the other sacraments of Initiation, Baptism and Eucharist) is hotly debated, the concern in this chapter will be more pastoral and catechetical. What is the impact of *The Challenge* on Confirmation preparation?

First let us look at what I consider to be a disturbing trend regarding preparation for Confirmation. There is an increasing tendency to substitute two-year preparation programs for the sacrament of Confirmation for a more comprehensive approach to ministry with youth, which includes a solid catechetical curriculum based on *The Challenge*. So many parish youth efforts are directed exclusively to Confirmation preparation. If the Church were to re-integrate Confirmation preparation and celebration into the initiatory sequence of Baptism-Confirmation-Eucharist (as had been celebrated prior to the 20th century), the vast majority of youth programs in the United States would cease to exist. *Outside of two-year Confirmation preparation programs, great numbers of parishes in the United States have no other ministry with youth—before or after Confirmation.* Many of these efforts are poorly conceived and offer no opportunities for continuing growth after Confirmation. It is no mystery why most youth resist these efforts and never return after Confirmation.

If you see some merit in my brief analysis, perhaps you will be ready to consider an alternative to the present situation. We have learned much about ministry with youth in the last ten years and now operate from a common vision (*Vision of Youth Ministry*, USCC, *The Challenge of Adolescent Catechesis*, NFCYM). I am offering the following guidelines in the hope that they will stir your thinking about Confirmation or support your current efforts to return Confirmation preparation to its place within a comprehensive youth ministry.

Guideline # 1

Focus on Building a Comprehensive Youth Ministry With a Solid Catechetical Curriculum

While two-year Confirmation programs provide a quick-fix to youth programming, the hard work of building a youth ministry is the challenge each parish must face. Developing a team of youth and adults, assessing youth needs, and developing a comprehensive and balanced ministry with youth that involves them are the keys. The *Vision of Youth Ministry* offers such a comprehensive framework for organizing a ministry with youth. It outlines the following primary components: Evangelization, Catechesis, Prayer and Worship, Justice, Peace and Service, Community Life, Guidance and Healing, Enablement (leadership development of youth and adults), and Advocacy. In addition, a parish which focuses on this approach will be able to situate Confirmation preparation within youth ministry. This comprehensive approach can serve as a foundation for celebrating Confirmation and continuing growth, placing the emphasis on ministry, not Confirmation.

Guideline # 2

Apply the Principles of Adolescent Catechesis to Confirmation Preparation

As we have seen, *The Challenge of Adolescent Catechesis* provides us with the key principles and faith themes for catechesis with younger and older adolescents. It offers a catechetical context within which to view Confirmation preparation. The faith themes for a catechetical curriculum outlined in this Manual can serve as a foundation prior to Confirmation catechesis and as a continuing catechesis after the celebration of the sacrament.

The principles outlined in *The Challenge* should be applied to Confirmation preparation. What would Confirmation preparation programs be like if they a) responded to the developmental, social and cultural needs of adolescents; b) respected the variability in maturation and learning needs of adolescents; c) respected the expanding freedom and autonomy of adolescents; d) used a variety of learning formats, environments, schedules and educational techniques; e) focused on particular faith themes in short term programming? Much of the current Confirmation programming would need to change.

Several implications emerge immediately. Respecting the variability in maturation and the expanding freedom of adolescents call into question Confirmation programs that confirm everyone of the same age or grade at the same time. People grow in faith at their own pace. How could every 15 or 16 year old be at the same point in faith growth or readiness for the sacrament? Careful consideration of *The Challenge* and the resources in this Manual will offer specific implications for your Confirmation practice.

Guideline # 3

Shorten Confirmation Preparation Programs to Six Months, Allowing Young People to Choose Freely When They Celebrate the Sacrament

I firmly believe we have to stop two year, mandatory, forced programs. These programs only serve to worsen the problem, not solve it. Let us shorten the sacramental preparation for Confirmation to six months, beginning in January and culminating in May/June. Let us celebrate the flow of the liturgical year from Lent through Easter to Pentecost in our preparation process. Such programming allows Confirmation programs to be modeled on the process of the RCIA (*Rite of Christian Initiation of Adults*), adapting the rituals (for example, the rite of enrollment) for Confirmation candidates. An outline of such a process is included in this chapter.

As an alternative to the two-year program, allow young people to choose when they are ready to celebrate the sacrament. How? Parishes can develop criteria for readiness that are based on a young person's participation in the youth ministry (and its programs) *and* on his or her faith growth during the adolescent years. By using youth ministry programming, a young person can prepare at his or her own pace for Confirmation by taking certain recommended catechetical courses from the catechetical program, participate in justice and service programming, plan and participate in worship experiences, learn how to pray, and belong to a community. In short, the youth ministry provides the context for growth in faith of *all* the young people of the parish, before or after a person celebrates Confirmation!

When a young person has completed the requirements developed by the parish, he or she then applies for the sacramental preparation program for Confirmation, is interviewed and begins the six month preparation process. By allowing young people to choose when they want to celebrate the sacrament, young people will not be confirmed as classes or grades. It allows then to prepare at their own pace, recognizing their freedom and the other involvements.

To handle the various routes that young people will take to Confirmation, a parish can develop a policy statement that outlines the preparation requirements, Confirmation process, and additional elements, like sponsors. The policy describes the recommended catechetical courses (or it could ask young people to select four courses from the eight that are offered), Justice and Service involvement, Worship and Prayer involvement, Community Life involvement and Retreat. The policy becomes the basis for helping young people develop their journey to Confirmation. A sample policy is included at the end of this chapter.

Guideline #4

Provide Continuing Opportunities for Growth and Ministry

Why do so many parishes offer nothing for young people once they have been confirmed? Most complain that the young people don't come back. I think this is a self-fulfilling prophecy. We tell them in any number of ways that Confirmation is the end of the line, we offer no opportunities for continuing growth, and then we wonder why they don't come back. Would you? If we focus on building a comprehensive youth ministry, we are going to the root of the problem.

We need to develop programs that focus on the new growth needs of those who have been confirmed. The confirmed young people need to have a say in what these programs will be and should be involved in planning them! One example of a program that can challenge youth is peer ministry—enabling youth to minister with their peers. Peer ministry can help young people live their faith which they celebrated in Confirmation.

Suggestions for Parish Confirmation Policies

A. Introduction and Rationale

- Important event for entire community

- Meaning of Confirmation (theological, attitudinal, impact on young person)

- Confirmation is not graduate or conclusion of involvmement in parish life.

B. Specific Policies

1. Readiness of Candidates

Parishes can develop criteria for readiness that are based on a young person's participation in the youth ministry (and its programs) *and* on his or her faith growth during the adolescent years. By using youth ministry programming, a young person can prepare at his or her own pace for Confirmation.

An Example of Participation Requirements

Catechetical courses: Prior to acceptance as a Confirmation candidate all the youth of our parish are required to take four of the following eight courses: Jesus, Gospels, Sexuality, Justice, Personal Growth, Moral Decision Making, Church, Relationships.

Service involvement: Prior to acceptance as a Confirmation candidate all the youth of our parish are required to participate in one service project lasting a full season or in three short-term projects.

Prayer and Worship: Prior to acceptance as a Confirmation candidate all the youth of our parish are required to join a liturgy planning team to plan and conduct a worship experience for all in youth ministry (for example, the Thanksgiving Eucharist).

These types of requirement could also be applied to involvement in the Guidance, Community Life, and Enablement components of youth ministry.

2. Confirmation Process

- Description of the program, length, schedule, liturgical events, catechetical content, retreat

- Role and Requirements for parents of those preparing to be confirmed

- Role and Requirements for sponsors

- Specify the role of participants in planning the Confirmation ceremony.

A Short-Term Confirmation Process Modeled on the RCIA

A. Basic Components of the Confirmation Process

1. Catechesis

Focused catechesis for the celebration of the sacrament of Confirmation.
Suggested themes: Sacraments of Initiation, Christian Lifestyle, Mission and Ministry of Jesus and the Church, Mission and Ministry of the Believer, Continuing Growth as a Christian.

2. Spiritual Formation

Suggested: Retreat experience on the spiritual life, learning to pray.

3. Liturgical/Ritual

Suggested: special celebrations of the Word and Eucharist during formation; special rites during formation process to mark the journey (Enrollment Ceremony); regular remembrance by the community.

C. Leadership Required for Successful Implementation of the Confirmation Process

A variety of leaders is needed for successful implementation of a Confirmation process. The following are suggested roles and responsibilities for a Confirmation team and its committees:

Team Coordinator

— coordinates/supervises the work of the team and committees
— convenes meetings and facilitates planning
— oversees recruitment, training, and supervision/support of leaders
— works with pastoral staff and other parish organizations to coordinate all aspects of the Confirmation program with total parish planning
— accountable for overall implementation of the Confirmation program.

B. Stages of Preparation Process Accommodated to the Liturgical Cycle
(6 month model)

January (Baptism of the Lord)	Invitation
January—Sunday before Lent	Interviews
First Sunday of Lent	Formal Inscription/enrollment
Lent	Confirmation Catechesis
Holy Week	Retreat Second Interviews
Easter	Renewal of Baptism Presentation to Community
Easter Season	Celebration of Confirmation
Pentecost Sunday	Special Liturgy Prepared by Newly Confirmed

Coordinator of Catechetical Program
— organizes/schedules catechetical component
— selects materials
— administers catechetical component
— provides for the formation of catechists
— convenes catechists for support/guidance
— assists catechists in their work.

Retreat Coordinator
— plans and organizes retreat experience
— recruits and trains staff for retreat experience

Liturgical Coordinator
— plans appropriate rites
— coordinates the liturgical aspects of the formation program.

Parent Involvement Coordinator
— plans/conducts orientation on Confirmation Program
— plans educational programs for parents
— invites parents to participate in appropriate aspects of Confirmation Program.

D. Planning a Confirmation Process

To assist you in planning a Confirmation process for your parish, the following planning suggestions are offered. [The "Curriculum Development Process" in Chapter 3 of this Manual can also assist you in developing the catechetical component of the Confirmation process.]

A. Preliminary decisions for planning
- How is the Confirmation Process integrated within the youth ministry and the adolescent catechesis curriculum?
- What is the length of the Confirmation process?
- What programs/opportunities will be provided for the young people after the Confirmation process?

B. Consider the elements for your overall plan
a. Letter of invitation

b. Evening of hospitality for parents and youth

c. Initial interview and concluding interview

d. Sponsor preparation

e. Catechetical program

f. Parental involvement/education program

g. Liturgical Component (Rite of Enrollment, Rite of Presentation, Rite of Confirmation).

C. Develop an overall calendar for the Confirmation process.
Outline in general form the flow of the various elements of the process. This will help the planners in creating programs to meet the expectations of the overall plan.

D. Develop each component of the Confirmation process using the committees.

E. Integrate the components into a holistic program
After the committees have developed the concrete programs, compile the individual programs and schedule them on the calendar. At this time any changes or renegotiating can take place. Each committee should also specify potential leaders for the program. The overall design should be presented to appropriate parish leadership for comment and/or approval.

F. Develop a comprehensive Confirmation policy for the parish

G. Develop your leadership system (recruiting/training/supporting leaders)

H. Promote/publicize the program throughout the parish

I. Implement the program
Schedule regular meetings of the Confirmation Team to monitor/coordinate the components of the program and to evaluate the progress of the program.

J. Evaluate the individual components, the overall program, and the work of the Confirmation team.

Notes

Notes

Notes

Notes